What O.

"*If Only: Letting Go of Regret* delivers deep wisdom wrapped in masterful writing, incisive insight, and relevant narrative. Michelle Van Loon's words continue to do their work long after the last page is turned. Her transparency cuts the core for everyone who has thought they've fallen short and struggled with regret. *If Only* delivers powerful tools to help readers grow, heal, and break free of the chains of the past."

—Shelly Beach, award-winning author,
The Silent Seduction of Self-Talk
and *Love Letters from the Edge*

"If only I had this book earlier in my life, I could've saved myself lots of guilt over past regrets and had the tools to live in such a way that I'd garner fewer of them. With an expert blend of raw, gutsy storytelling, biblical, tried-and-true wisdom, and some 'did you read my soul?' prayers to bring it all home, Michelle Van Loon shows us all how to live beyond the 'if onlys' and accept the grace and love that await."

—Caryn Rivadeneira, author
Broke: What Financial Desperation Revealed About God's Abundance
and *Known and Loved: 52 Devotions from the Psalms*

"So many of us ruefully pine over our various roads not traveled. In *If Only* Michelle Van Loon offers gentle wisdom from Scripture and moving stories that show us how we can own our regrets so that they don't own and consume us, inviting us to live in the freedom for which Christ set us free."

—Rachel Marie Stone, author
Eat with Joy: Redeeming God's Gift of Food

"Regret can debilitate us. Paralyze us. Imprison us in a shriveling life. Michelle Van Loon knows what it's like to live in regret and with its accompanying miseries. But, no more. Now she lives the Jesus life to the full. In this warmly rich and insightful book, Michelle becomes for us God's messenger of grace, one who helps us unlock our prison doors. Read this book and be set free to live the abundant life Jesus offers. Stick with this eminently wise companion. I can think of no better guide to lead us from regret to redemption."

—Marlena Graves, author
A Beautiful Disaster: Finding Hope in the Midst of Brokenness

"If only . . . I could make sense of all the stuff that either hasn't happened, won't happen, or can't happen. Regrets come 24/7, and Michelle helps us choose a journey that releases us from our resentments over life's missing pieces."

—Melinda Schmidt, broadcaster
co-host, "Midday Connection,"
Moody Radio Network

"Michelle Van Loon writes with sensitivity, biblical insight, and touching humor about something that is painfully present in all of our lives. *If Only* addresses a topic that can either overwhelm us or paralyze us. She helps us understand regret, see it clearly, and deal with it appropriately. This book will be a much-needed resource, especially for women, and will help many untangle the webs of regret that have held us captive for years. I highly recommend this very special book."

—Dale Hanson Bourke, author
Embracing Your Second Calling

"In *If Only*, Michelle Van Loon not only acknowledges the weight of guilt most of us privately carry, but parses the difference between remorse and regret. More importantly, she invites readers to redeem our 'if onlys.' Convicting, confessional, and grace-filled, Van Loon's words will nudge readers toward letting go of regret and toward loving God and others with a whole heart. I love the stories she tells and the wisdom she imparts in this compelling book."

—Jennifer Grant, author
Love You More,
MOMumental,
Disquiet Time,
and *12.*

IF ONLY

IF ONLY
LETTING GO OF REGRET

BY
MICHELLE VAN LOON

BEACON HILL PRESS
OF KANSAS CITY

Beacon Hill Press of Kansas City
PO Box 419527
Kansas City, MO 64141
www.BeaconHillBooks.com

ISBN 978-0-8341-3250-4

Printed in the
United States of America

The Internet addresses, email addresses, and phone numbers in this book are accu-
rate at the time of publication. They are provided as a resource. Beacon Hill Press of
Kansas City does not endorse them or vouch for their content or permanence.

Cover Design: Ryan Deo
Interior Design: Sharon Page

Library of Congress Cataloging-in-Publication Data
Van Loon, Michelle.
 If only : letting go of regret / Michelle Van Loon.
  pages cm
 Includes bibliographical references.
 ISBN 978-0-8341-3250-4 (pbk.)
 1. Regret—Religious aspects—Christianity. I. Title.
 BV4909.V35 2014
 248.8'6—dc23

                                                    2014012024

10 9 8 7 6 5 4 3 2 1

CONTENTS

ACKNOWLEDGMENTS

Have you ever had a time in your life when it seemed you kept having the same conversation over and over again? It was this way for me about the topic of regret. After a while, I recognized God was at work in dozens of conversations I had with women ranging in age from early twenties through seventy-plus. My first thank you goes to each person who shared her struggle with "if only" with me and gave me the privilege of sharing a bit of my own in return.

A big "thanks" goes to the team at Beacon Hill, who believed in the message of this book. It has been a joy and an honor working with each one of you.

I am grateful to Meg Kausalik, Dr. Kathy Bogacz, and Carol Marshall, who volunteered to read much of the first draft of this manuscript. First drafts are never pretty, but they managed to hear what I was trying to say despite the messes I sent them, and their prayers, questions, and feedback helped me clarify my thoughts. If this book makes sense, it is due to their input.

Proverbs 15:23 says, "How good is a timely word!" Karen Neumair's encouragement to flesh this idea out into a book proposal, Dr. John Hawthorne's November 21, 2013, blog post about corporate regret, and Katherine Willis Pershey's inspired title suggestion were all timely words during the writing of this book. Diane Siri's counsel was another sort of timely word for me; God used her skilled listening and insight to bring order to my heart's chaos at a crossroads time in my life.

My fellow contributors at *Christianity Today's* Her.meneutics blog and an additional online group of scribes who write about faith offered me cheerleading, prayer, and a few "aha!" moments. Each of these women has encouraged me by example to reach beyond what is comfortable in my thinking and writing. They've been used by God to shape my soul as well as my words.

My children have lived so many of the stories I told in this book. Gabriel and Lio are lights in my life, and it is my highest joy to be their grandma. I love each one of you more than you could ever imagine.

My beloved husband, Bill, has listened to me talk through ideas and then read those ideas again when I wrote them, encouraged me to keep going through years when it seemed that no one wanted to read what I wrote, and has prayed for and with me. "Thank you" and "I love you" seem like such meager words to offer you. I could not have done this without you, and I wouldn't have wanted to.

Finally and first of all, I am in awe of the transforming work of my Messiah Jesus. He is indeed making all things new.

INTRODUCTION

For months on end, it seemed as though every conversation I had with friends, workplace acquaintances, or the checker at the grocery store included one of them using the two saddest words in the English language.

"If only."

"If only I would have gotten a second opinion . . ."

"If only I would have listened to my children . . ."

"If only I would have listened to my parents . . ."

"If only I would have asked for help . . ."

"If only I would have done something to help . . ."

"If only I would have said no . . ."

"If only I could have said yes . . ."

I was tuned to the frequency of those two little words in these conversations because I'd been singing harmony to their blues song in the key of me. I'd been successfully ignoring my own regrets for years, choosing instead to warehouse them in a distant corner of my heart. Perhaps I imagined that they'd just quietly disintegrate over time. Perhaps I didn't believe that there was a place for them if I was doing my best to live the victorious Christian life. Or maybe I was just too busy to notice my regrets were stacking up like trash bags during a garbage strike.

As I approached midlife, I discovered that my internal warehouse was running out of space.

I wasn't the only one. The choir singing sad songs of lament seemed to be made up of lots of women in my age group. But they weren't the only ones. I heard from one woman nearly twice my age. Younger women just launching into adulthood. Teens.

The pain of regret overwhelmed them to the point of deep depression. Others coped by throwing all of their energies into performance, trying to convince others they were not just OK, they were *fabulous*. There were a few others who discovered that their "if only" list was a catalyst that spurred them toward real spiritual and emotional growth.

Few of us walk through life without accumulating regret. At some point, our past choices collide with the reality that there is no do-over button in life. Those two little words—"if only"—shackle us to a life that falls short of the freedom and joy promised us by Jesus. Mary Shelley, the author of *Frankenstein*, once observed that regret causes us to become "cannibals of our own hearts." Unresolved regret is a leech that steals from our present in order to feed the pain of our past, hindering our future in the process.

Meet the "If Only" Family

The "If Only" family has two "siblings." Their names are "Regret" and "Remorse."

Regret is our awareness of the consequences of an event or action. We experience a sense of loss in the wake of a poor or painful choice we've made as we realize what has followed in the wake of that decision: "I wish I wouldn't have eaten that cold pizza out of the office refrigerator for breakfast because I felt like puking for the rest of the day." Bible teacher Warren Wiersbe summed up the essence of regret with a single question: "Why did I do that?"

Remorse reflects our sense of moral guilt at our own (real or perceived) failure. It speaks to our emotional distress about our choices and has to do with our sorrow over the choice itself, rather than the consequences: "I shouldn't have stolen that cold pizza out of the office refrigerator and eaten it for breakfast because it didn't belong to me."

Remorse and regret bleed into each other in the same way blue and violet merge on a rainbow. It is helpful to understand the distinctions, but it is also important to remember that the two work in tandem in our lives. We do something we regret, and we feel remorse about it. If we act on that remorse, it can lead us forward to a new course of action.

Our regrets, on the other hand, shove our emotional gearshift into reverse.

In Western culture, we face an endless buffet of choices every day: everything from what school our kids will attend to what outfit we'll wear to a dizzying menu of church choices to which kind of toppings we'd like to order on our next pizza. Choosing one thing means excluding others. Researchers who have studied regret learned that the more choices we have before us, the more opportunities we have to accumulate regrets.

Regret researchers from the University of Illinois–Champaign and Northwestern University queried 370 adults about their most memorable regrets.[1] Almost 20 percent of respondents reported they had a regret about a romantic relationship. Sixteen percent shared stories of family issues and an additional 9 percent cited specific parenting mistakes. Other categories of regret included education, vocation, financial decisions, and health choices. A recent LifeWay study[2] found that nearly half of those polled said they were currently dealing with the consequences of an earlier bad decision.

Redeeming Regret

Jesus promises his followers something better than a do-over. He promises a new life (John 3:1-21). Paul echoed this promise when he told his friends at Corinth, "If anyone is in Christ, the new creation has come: The old has gone, the new is here!" (2 Cor. 5:17).

We may sing that God's grace is amazing, that we once were lost and now are found. Our churches encourage us toward bold faith and celebrate stories of transformation. So we wonder what is wrong with us because we may still be lugging around lingering regrets from our lives before we came to faith in him. Or we feel ashamed because we've managed to rack up a regret tab in the time since we've been found.

And the situation isn't helped when those of us who've battled regret are met with breezy certainty that regret should be a nonissue. "You're forgiven . . . period," these people insist. "Your regrets should no longer have any power over you now that you're in Christ."

If only it were always that simple.

Denying that our regrets exist is a setup for spiritual frustration. It is a recipe for a divided heart. On one side of the divide is the life we think we're supposed to be living. On the other side is our regrets. Christ indeed makes all things new. He is at work to reunite our divided hearts. This means that he will reclaim, redeem, and repurpose every single one of our regrets as we submit ourselves to his work in our lives. In light of our regrets, we can pray: "Teach me your way, Lord, that I may rely on your faithfulness; give me an undivided heart, that I may fear your name" (Ps. 86:11).

I'd learned to ignore my own list titled "If Only" until the weight of my regrets threatened to collapse the place I'd stored and ignored them for years. I didn't realize how those regrets owned me. That prayer was the beginning of a wonderful journey toward freedom for me, though I didn't realize it the first time I prayed it. I'm journeying with Jesus out of that dark warehouse-sized prison of regrets.

It's a journey to which he's inviting you too.

This book is meant to help you respond to his invitation. It features true stories of regret—my own as well as the stories of others. (Names and some details have been changed due to the sometimes-sensitive nature of the events I'm recounting.) It also features thoughtful, fresh, and faithful application of Scripture's truth. The stories and Scripture are meant to give you what I've heard called "the gift of going second." The stories may prompt you to consider your own choices in new ways or give you new ways of talking about regret with others you know. Each chapter ends with a few reflection questions and a prayer. It is a resource you can use on your own or in a small group.

I also recognize that there are some who have regrets so deeply entrenched and traumatic that you may need the help of a trained professional to work through them. The appendix at the back of the book has some resources if you find you need that help. Know that your regrets must not have the final word in your life.

That's my prayer for every reader. I believe with my whole heart that if you're holding the book in your hands, you're longing to know if it's possible for your deepest regrets to be redeemed.

They can. God does.

If only . . .

ONE

WOULDA, COULDA, SHOULDA VERSUS ME

RECOGNIZING REGRET

> Of all the words of mice and men, the saddest are,
> "It might have been."
> —Kurt Vonnegut

:ing in a busy fast food joint at lunchtime with my three :ids. One moment, I was eating an order of french fries; the next, without warning, I began to sob. It was not a dignified, gentle, Jane Austen-heroine light mist that could be staunched with a clean lace hankie, but a full-on blubber that soon included snot ribbons dripping from my chin.

My three preteen kids could do nothing but inhale the rest of their burgers in awkward silence while simultaneously hoping that the ground would open up and swallow them alive so they didn't have to die of embarrassment. The one saving grace of this awkward moment was that the kids thought that my tears were a result of a traumatic event that had happened in our living room a couple of hours earlier.

I didn't have words to explain to them that the painful episode had almost instantly drained a decade-old well of sorrow buried inside of me; exposing a deep regret, polished diamond-bright by the passing of time.

I couldn't ignore my regret any longer, nor could I re-bury it. It was too big. Though I thought I'd learned to live with it, in the restaurant that day I realized that I'd done little more than make a truce with my regret.

Jesus didn't add a regret clause when he promised his followers abundant life ("I have come that they may have life, and have it to the full" [John 10:10]) that read "except in cases where the party of the second part has stumbled, struggled, or sinned."

It didn't much matter. I'd penciled in the clause myself.

Dismissing Remorse

We do something we regret, and we feel remorse about it. Those who follow Christ trust that his life, death, and resurrection save us from our sins, but he often uses the consequences of those sins to refine us. If we don't allow our remorse to help us recognize those consequences for what they are, they can become a perfect breeding ground for regret.

Just a couple of hours before my midday meltdown, I had placed our first foster baby into the long-waiting arms of her adoptive mother. I'd brought Rhiannon home from the hospital and cared for her night and day for the first six weeks of her life. I'd known from the start she was headed for a wonderful adoptive family's home, but I realized that the only way I'd be able to be a good foster mother was to be a good mom. I needed to care for this child as if she were my own.

While this no-holds-barred love was the best possible way for Rhiannon to begin her life, it was a perfect recipe for a broken heart for me.

After I'd placed the baby into the arms of her adoptive mom, my kids and I shed some tears as we all said good-bye to Rhiannon and wished her new family well. But as we sat in the restaurant at lunch, sorrow's drill hit my soul's bedrock. At the time, I credited my public breakdown to the obvious: I'd just said good-bye to a little baby who had snuggled into me and fell asleep against my heart with the kind of trust that only a completely dependent newborn is capable of. She'd given me her first toothless smiles in return.

Rhiannon's departure was a trigger, to be sure. But my deep grief overflowed as I looked at my own three kids at the restaurant that day and realized how very quickly our time together was passing. I was a little more than midway through my active parenting years. Perhaps a perceptive counselor would have suggested to me that deciding to foster newborns was my way of trying to hold onto the past. I would have gone the counselor one better. I would have told him or her that I wasn't trying to recapture my past. I was trying to rewrite it in order to erase one of my deepest regrets.

The seeds of my sorrow were planted almost ten years earlier. July 25, 1986—a red-letter day, the day my youngest child was born. It should have been one of the most joyful days of my life.

It was, and it was one of the saddest, too. My husband, Bill, and I had decided during that pregnancy that three children were enough. Enough, as in, "I really couldn't handle another slice of that triple-chocolate cheesecake. I'm stuffed." We were about to have our third baby in as many years, and we were stuffed. More accurately, we were depleted by the daily marathon of life with three children under three.

We'd avoided the topic of our decision in our prayers to God. We never asked him his opinion about our family size. Instead, we told one another we just couldn't handle any more. Three kids were enough.

My tubal ligation was scheduled for the day our youngest was born. "It's easier to do the procedure right after a birth," my obstetrician had explained.

After Jacob was born, I was wheeled into surgery, still high on the ecstasy of a healthy birth and meeting our beautiful, peaceful little boy. As the surgical team was doing their prep work, my obstetrician—the man who'd delivered my baby just a couple of hours earlier—stopped and looked intently at me.

"You know, you don't have to do this," he said after a pregnant moment. "Are you sure you're ready to go ahead with the procedure?"

I've always wondered what prompted him to ask that question. Maybe he asked it of all of his young patients. I was only twenty-seven years old at the time. One thing I do know: his question felt as if the voice of God had tried to preempt my regularly scheduled program.

My mind raced: What would Bill say if I backed out now? How would we handle whatever it was that was coming next? The babies seemed to be coming fast and furious in our household, and our other attempts to slow the flow had not been successful. My courage was at an all-time low.

I well knew the Scripture passage that affirmed that children were a gift from God:

Children are a heritage from the LORD, offspring a reward from him. Like arrows in the hands of a warrior are children born in one's youth. Blessed is the man whose quiver is full of them. They will not be put to shame when they contend with their opponents in court. (Ps. 127:3-5)

In theory, I affirmed the truth of these words. I had the distinct sense that obeying God in that moment meant telling the doctor not to go ahead with the tubal ligation. Not that day. Probably not ever.

I had no idea how I was supposed to walk out this obedience in real time, so I reverted to my default setting. I did what seemed right in my own eyes.

I looked away from the doctor's gaze. "I'm sure. Do it." God's voice fell silent as the anesthesiologist put the mask over my face. The world went black.

I didn't have time to process the regret of that moment for months. Life was overflowing with the demands of our young family. One warm summer day, as I was watching my kids splash in the inflatable kiddie pool in our tiny backyard, remorse hit me like a freight train. I'd never be pregnant again.

What had I done? I had a sudden, heart-stopping moment as I wondered if I'd committed an unforgivable sin. The next moment, I was certain I had because I didn't think I'd ever be able to forgive myself. When I confessed my deep regret to my husband, he confessed that he'd had a few guilt pangs of his own about our decision. A note here: our individual convictions on this subject are not prescriptions for the decisions of others. Our regret had much to do with making a long-term, permanent decision about our family based on our changeable emotions at the time instead of prayerful deliberation.

We learned that the tubal had left me with female plumbing problems. I had scarred inside after the procedure. If I hadn't committed the unpardonable sin, I certainly managed to indulge in an irreversible one.

My unresolved guilt festered for nearly a decade. When we began attending a church populated by a number of adoptive and foster families, I wondered if God had hit the family reset button for us. The finances required for adoption were daunting, to say the least, but we thought we could try foster parenting and see where it took us. Our kids were excited at the prospect of having a little baby come to live with us for a while. The social worker that evaluated our family and home prior to granting us a foster license told us we were a perfect family for the task.

She knew this was going to be a part of our family's ministry but had no idea that foster care was both penance and prayer for me. My unvoiced hope was that maybe one of the foster babies would be left with us—things like that happened once in a while, I knew—and it would be a sign that God really had forgiven me and that I was worthy to mother another child in spite of my decision to have a tubal ligation a decade earlier.

My grief in the restaurant the day Rhiannon left us was sadness at letting her go, but also a revelatory moment when I began to come to terms with the fact that I could not go back to fix the past. My regret had long anchored me to that single disobedient moment in time. My response to the remorse I felt was to beat myself up with my failure in my own wrongheaded attempt to somehow make myself right with God. I wanted so much to be able to right my wrong, to turn my "if only" into a do-over.

I felt a new wave of sorrow as I accepted the fact that there were not going to be any do-overs in this area of my life. Jesus had been waiting and working through all of this to free me from my self-punishment habit. That fresh sorrow marked the reality that I'd finally begun to surrender to God by allowing remorse to do its work in me. The Message paraphrase of 2 Corinthians 7:10 explains the work of this kind of godly sorrow: "Distress that drives us to God does that. It turns us around. It gets us back in the way of salvation. We never regret that kind of pain. But those who let distress drive them away from God are full of regrets, end up on a deathbed of regrets."

I also began to discover that day how our loving God can redeem our regrets.

The Past on "Repeat"

Regret serves a training purpose in our lives. One of the first things newborns discover is that their cry creates a response from the world: warm milk, comforting arms, a dry diaper. This cause-and-effect interaction with the world teaches babies how the world works.

It doesn't take long before we graduate to some version of the old "the dog ate my homework" dodge to avoid uncomfortable short-term consequences. As we move toward adulthood, one of our greatest strengths is our idealism. The passion that fuels our idealism also feeds idealism's trigger-happy pal—impulsiveness. When we're young, we're prone to making quick decisions without considering long-term consequences. As a result, we're also prone to accumulating a nice collection of unprocessed regrets that we may not fully realize until we approach midlife.

I wonder how many times Adam and Eve replayed the moment they bit into the forbidden fruit throughout the rest of their long lives (Gen. 3:1-7) or how many times Esau cursed himself for his impatience at trading his inheritance and his father's blessing for a bowl of lentils (Gen. 25:24-34). Judas's regret at betraying his friend Jesus drove him to suicide (Matt. 27:1-5).

In the weeks after my lunchtime meltdown, I took a small first step in facing my regrets by intentionally choosing not to keep hitting the "repeat" button on my decision. I wanted to be intentional about reflecting on the good God had brought into my life despite my bad choices, something I really hadn't done very often. The exercise offered me a new appreciation for the sovereignty of God. If it is true that God weaves all things together for both our good and his glory (Rom. 8:28), then it follows that he is able to redeem our sinful decisions in order to serve his purposes. I realized that while my life may have been less fruitful as a result of the consequences of my choice, it hadn't been exactly barren. Mothering three beautiful children, helping my husband as he finished college while working full time, caring for friends, doing the work God had given me, learning, serving in a couple of meaningful ministry roles—each one bore the imprint of eternity. The exercise didn't instantly erase every regret, but it did serve to interrupt the unhealthy cycle of self-recrimination in which I'd been trapped with some spiritually nourishing, God-glorifying thanksgiving.

Pausing my endless loop of "if only" opened my ears to the lyrics of that tired song to which I'd been dancing and dancing and dancing. It was time to learn some new steps.

Reflection Questions

1. What are some of your longest-standing regrets?

2. In what ways can you see how your past regrets have affected your present life? How do they shape the way you think about your future?

3. What is one positive thing that has happened in your life as a result of a past regret?

4. If you were going to write a letter to a younger version of you just before you made a decision you now know would lead to regret, what would you say to yourself? What do you think God might say to that younger version of you?

Prayer

O my Redeemer, here I am. Regrets and all.

I am sensing how my own collection of "if onlys" tethers me to the past. I have beaten myself up with the past I thought would please you better than the past I have lived. Maybe I believed you would have been there somehow more fully in that perfect past I've dreamed for myself. I'm sorry for thinking so foolishly. You are Lord, and there is nowhere I've been that is a surprise to you.

You never intended me to carry the baggage of my past into my present. Help me to recognize the baggage, Lord. And help me to drop it, then turn those empty palms to you in surrender. It is only from a place of surrender that you can come to set me free from the prison of my regrets so I can follow you fully, wholeheartedly, and fearlessly into the future.

Please teach me some new steps, the ones that will help me follow you out of this place of regret in which I've been living. I pray this in the name of the One who came to set captives free.

Amen.

TWO

OH, THE PLACES WE GO!

HIDING FROM THE SINS WE COMMIT

Of all words of tongue and pen, the saddest are,
"It might have been."

—Bret Harte

• •

The Great Physician doled out a full-octane remedy to people who were convinced they were pictures of health and spiritual vitality. He was not mixing his healing words with a spoonful of sugar so the medicine would go down more easily. He gave it to them straight.

Jesus told a number of stories to the "healthy" religious authorities of his day in an attempt to describe his relationship with the raggedy sinners they excelled at avoiding at all costs. They had to protect themselves from the people who carried the plague of sin, believing that this would immunize them from coming down with a case of impurity or being left with a lingering case of regret.

If only it were as simple as that.

The religious elites believed they were doing God a favor by avoiding the people carrying the disease of sin. They didn't recognize that they were carriers too. In their eyes, the foolish Jesus who spent time with them may as well have thrown himself into a roomful of people who each had a live case of typhoid, smallpox, Ebola, and lice.

In response, Jesus demonstrated his "foolishness" and showed off his Father's wholehearted love for all sinners by his actions (touching sick people! eating with scandalous people! oy!) and with his words. He asked his hearers to see with fresh eyes the character of the God they insisted they were serving with their harsh rules and loveless ways. He wanted them to remember that they were called long ago by God to reflect his light to the world (Deut. 4:5-8).

Of all the stories Jesus told, there is none more beloved and familiar than the parable of the prodigal son found in Luke 15:11-32. Imagine if you were someone who'd worked overtime to avoid the contagion of sin and the scarring of regret when you heard these words. At first, Jesus draws you in with a morality tale that seems to celebrate your careful lifestyle.

And then, an "if only" moment makes an appearance in the story and changes everything.

The Stink of the Pigpen

As the curtain rises on the story Jesus told, we meet a strong, über-confident young man bursting at his own seams to get out there and make his mark on the great big world. He'd convinced himself he'd never be able to star in his own life as long as he was chained to his father's provincial business and color-in-the-lines ways.

This young man paced like a pent-up bull behind his father's house as he rehearsed the most important speech of his young life. "Give me my share of the estate" (Luke 15:12). He wanted right now what would have eventually been his when his father died.

Jesus doesn't give us any background to why the younger man in his story demanded his share of the money in that moment, but his description of the young man's subsequent actions certainly shone a light on his motivations: "Not long after that, the younger son got together all he had, set off for a distant country and there squandered his wealth in wild living" (v. 13).

If I were to put this young man's thought process into my own words, it would sound something like this: "I deserve to get out of this house, this town. I deserve to party with the high rollers. I deserve to have sex, and I will use my father's money to pay for it. I am taking care of me!"

When his poorly invested shekels run out, shame kicks in as the young man heads to a pig farm in order to survive. The irony of this destination wasn't wasted on any of Jesus' Jewish hearers, who knew that pork was unclean, not kosher (Lev. 11:1-8). The religious experts hearing this story must have had a moment at this point where they were cheering inside: "See? This is what you get when you don't follow the rules!" This young man had left the security of family to travel to a distant land to do things his way. Now he was so desperate that he'd sunk to eating the food that these unclean animals were eating. He had to grub for food as if he were just another animal.

In his quest to make his mark, the young man had spent his financial inheritance, as well as his relational and spiritual one. His hunger and his degraded lifestyle sliced the long string of rationalizations he'd applied to his life that had gotten him to this point. Regret about his choices awakened him to the cumulative effect of his sin, when he realized that even the high-fiber diet of husks that served as pig food looked like a feast to him (Luke 15:16).

In that moment, "he came to his senses" (v. 17). This fictional young man allowed himself to remember the kind of man his father was. He hoped his father would be true to his compassionate character and give him a job. He'd spent his future.

You can imagine the young man in the story trudging homeward, rehearsing aloud the speech he's going to give his father. He prepared to confess his list of sins against God and his father, and ask his father for a job. Before he could deliver one line of his speech, "While he was still a long way off, his father saw him and was filled with compassion for him; he ran to his son, threw his arms around him and kissed him" (v. 20). In the grip of his father's embrace, the son attempts to confess. The father isn't interested in the son's recitation of his sins. The father welcomes him home as his once-lost, now-found son. He clothes the young man in garments meant to eradicate the stink of pig and regret, and he throws him a party.

At this point in the story, Jesus' religious audience was probably getting a little angry. That rotten young man didn't merit any special consideration from his father! Why would Jesus send the ingrate back home? And why would this father welcome him as if he were a war hero instead of a scoundrel? Just what was Jesus trying to say here?

Come to think of it, they heard Jesus loud and clear. They didn't like a syllable of this heartwarming welcome home scene.

To make matters worse, this wasn't even the end of this story. Jesus continued to challenge their regularly scheduled religious program as he told them about this father's other son—a son his hearers would have celebrated as one of their own. We'll be picking up his story in a later chapter.

Am I This Guy?

Most of us are able to recognize our own "younger son" tendencies to some degree. Even if we suspect that we might have more in common with Jesus' audience of religious professionals than with the younger brother in the parable, author Henri Nouwen offers us a helpful mirror that should help us see a younger brother with your name and mine looking back at us:

> I am the prodigal son every time I search for unconditional love where it cannot be found . . . Why do I keep leaving home where I am called a child of God, the Beloved of my Father? I am constantly surprised at how I keep taking the gifts God has given me—my health, my intellectual and emotional gifts— and keep using them to impress people, receive affirmation and praise, and compete for rewards, instead of developing them for the glory of God. Yes, I often carry them off to a "distant country" and put them in the service of an exploiting world that does not know their true value. It's almost as if I want to prove to myself and to my world that I do not need God's love, that I can make a life on my own, that I want to be fully independent. Beneath it all is the great rebellion, the radical "No" to the Father's love, the unspoken curse: "I wish you were dead." The prodigal son's "No" reflects Adam's original rebellion: his rejection of the God in whose love we are created and by whose love we are sustained . . . It is the rebellion that makes me dissipate myself in a "distant country."[1]

Nouwen's words remind me that I don't have to travel far to find myself in a distant country. I amaze myself at my seemingly unlimited capacity to keep buying myself tickets there.

During the last twenty-four hours, I've gossiped, I've lied, I've attempted to manipulate another person in order to get them to serve my selfish needs, rather than asking what is best for them. I've been a glutton. I've wallowed in self-pity. I have not gone the second mile to help someone in need . . . or the first mile, for that matter. No doubt, there are a few more sins I've committed in the last day that I've already forgotten.

In lieu of seeking God's forgiveness and, in some cases, additionally seeking the forgiveness of someone I may have bulldozed with my sin, sometimes I resort to taking a spiritual shortcut—or three. I don't need to take that journey back home to my heavenly Father if I can figure out a way to stay put in my distant land by finding an excuse for my actions:

- "It wasn't really gossip. I was just trying to let you know what was happening in our neighborhood by sharing the story of how the kid next door ended up in rehab."
- "I needed to eat that half-gallon of praline crunch ice cream straight from the carton at 11:30 p.m. because I skipped breakfast and lunch today. Besides, I had a really hard day and I deserve a treat."
- "When I got that call from my friend looking for emergency babysitting help, I didn't want the inconvenience, so I stretched the truth about my schedule just a bit. I *am* really busy, and I'm sure she'll find someone else to lend her a hand."

When we make excuses for our sinful behavior, we're attempting to protect ourselves from negative consequences–or the pain of "if only." Rationalizing our sins is one tried-and-true way of blessing our wrong desires and excusing our poor choices. And it can propel us far from home.

What We Have Coming to Us

I once asked a gracious, humble older man nearing the end of his life about what he dreamed for himself when he was a young man. I knew the headlines of his story: he'd gone through two messy divorces, lost custody of his kids from the first marriage, and lived with another woman for a while before she kicked him out. He was an alcoholic and spent years bouncing from job to job before he landed on the streets for a time.

"I certainly had some big ideas about what I was going to be," he said. "I thought the world owed me something. But when I look back, there was only one decision that pulled me off God's path for my life. You know what? I don't even remember exactly what it was, but I do believe that the first time I told myself I *deserved* to do what I wanted to do even though I knew it was dead wrong, I got myself going in the wrong direction."

Minimizing our sin by telling ourselves we deserve to do what we want to do even if it's wrong gives us plenty of momentum to launch us off that narrow path journey to which God calls us (Matt. 7:13-14). Rationalization makes a lousy GPS.

My friend Connie had been using that GPS for quite some time before she revealed where it had led her.

"I'm planning to leave Mike," she told me after church one Sunday.

Whoa. I didn't see that one coming. I'd long admired the sense of affection and teamwork between the pair.

"God told me that I never should have married Mike." There wasn't a whiff of uncertainty in her statement. She could have been reading me the phone book.

I groped for a response. "But you've been married for more than twenty-five years."

She shrugged and stared out the window. "Our marriage was a mistake from day one." Connie said she and Mike had been faithful to one another. She told me there had never been a hint of physical abuse between them, and neither one had any addiction issues clouding the picture. "None of that matters," she said. "The bottom line is that God wants me to be happy and Mike has never made me happy. I'm fifty-one years old. It's now or never."

. . . And Out Jumped This Golden Calf

In order to convince ourselves that we're doing the right thing even when we know it's the wrong thing, we engage in this thing called cognitive dissonance. Author Gabriel Garnica explains cognitive dissonance this way:

> People dislike inconsistency, or dissonance, between their actions and beliefs. This aversion to dissonance is so great that people will go as far as changing their beliefs to justify their actions and decisions and soothe their conscience . . . People will rationalize behavior they inherently know may be bad until they convince themselves that the behavior is acceptable, justified, or moral.[2]

I don't know what was going on behind closed doors at Mike and Connie's house. When I asked her if she thought marriage counseling might help, she rolled her eyes. "No. Marriage counseling is for people who want to try to save their marriages. I don't."

Exodus 32 offers us a great example of cognitive dissonance. Moses had recently led Israel's children out of slavery in Egypt. God called Moses up to Mount Sinai for an extended meeting. Moses' brother Aaron was left in charge of the people while he was away.

Anyone who has ever parented a toddler with a case of separation anxiety will recognize the reaction of an entire nation of people when Moses was gone a little longer than they thought he should be. En masse, they freaked out and demanded that Aaron bring back their "old-time Egyptian religion" by creating some gods they could worship just like their former masters used to do. Their logic in this moment of crisis was a perfect example of rationalization. Their need for immediate comfort trumped the lessons they'd learned about the God of Abraham, Isaac, and Jacob in the weeks and months preceding Moses' departure.

Aaron's rationalization mind-set was on full display as he responded to their plea. He told the people to give him all the gold earrings in their possession. He then cast the precious metal into the

34

image of a calf and introduced the idol to the people as their new god, the one who'd delivered them from the Egyptians. The calf was an image that would have been familiar to them, as their former captors had a god who looked exactly like the creature Aaron crafted.

God sent Moses back to the people, carrying stone tablets God had chiseled with Ten Commandments. (It is worth noting here that the first word of those commandments to the people was "You shall have no other gods before me" [Exod. 20:3; see vv. 3-4]). Moses turned out to be the ultimate party crasher, as he threw the stone tablets down in fury. He pulverized the golden statue into powder, mixed it with water, and made the people drink it. In the heat of the desert, the remnants of their golden god would work its way through every Israelite's digestive tract.

When Moses confronted Aaron, Aaron's case of cognitive dissonance was exposed for what it was. His recounting of the facts makes it sound as though he was just trying to help the people, like anyone in his place with half a heart would have done. He was just as surprised as Moses was that a calf magically appeared in the midst of the people (never mind that he'd sculpted the calf himself):

You know how prone these people are to evil. They said to me, "Make us gods who will go before us. As for this fellow Moses who brought us up out of Egypt, we don't know what has happened to him." So I told them, "Whoever has any gold jewelry, take it off." Then they gave me the gold, and I threw it into the fire, and out came this calf! (Exod. 32:22-24)

Every time I read this account, I wonder how Aaron said this with a straight face. Voila! Out came this calf!

It was no joke. In his mercy, God disciplined his people in order to show them how their actions offended him. In his mercy, he once again schooled Aaron on who he was, is, and would always be to his people.

35

Feeling the Burn

What peels away our carefully constructed rationalizations? What pierces our ways of soothing the discomfort of our cognitive dissonance?

Both of these self-protective responses act as shock absorbers and sin buffers in our lives. And both can be remarkably effective at preventing us from feeling regret.

God's discipline of us is designed to help us acknowledge and disconnect from those responses so we can, like the younger son in the parable, pack our rags and head toward home. As uncomfortable as they may be, our regrets may be a sign that we're responding to God's work in our lives. And that work includes recognizing our sin for what it is—an affront to our pure, holy, beautiful God and a toxin that infects our relationships with others and with ourselves.

The writer of Hebrews recognizes that God's discipline is for our ultimate benefit, even if it smarts in the moment and even if it hurts for a bunch of moments after that. "God disciplines us for our good, in order that we may share in his holiness. No discipline seems pleasant at the time, but painful. Later on, however, it produces a harvest of righteousness and peace for those who have been trained by it" (Heb. 12:10-11).

A few years after Connie divorced Mike and moved out of the area, I ran into her daughter. She told me that Connie had come to regret her decision to leave Mike. "Back then, my mom was not in a good place with God or with herself. She convinced herself that all of her problems were my dad's fault," she said. Mike had recently remarried, so there was no putting Mike and Connie's broken marriage back together again.

Connie's new life hadn't brought her the bliss she expected it would. When God didn't deliver on the happiness she thought he'd promised her, she disconnected herself from him too. The last time I'd spoken with Connie, nearly three years earlier, she told me as much.

I reflected on the years of pain this family had experienced. I hoped Connie's regrets were a sign that she was ready to take the same journey out of the distant land that the younger son in Jesus' parable did. I prayed Connie was heading homeward into the welcoming arms of her heavenly Father.

There are plenty of routes to that distant land. Some journeys are dramatic, like that of the parable's party-hard younger son's or Connie's determined dismantling of her marriage. Some journeys there are a little like driving across North Dakota at thirty-five miles per hour. But they often begin with a choice to do something God has asked us not to do.

And sometimes, that choice looks a whole lot like doing nothing at all.

Reflection Questions

1. In what areas of your life are you most tempted to rationalize your sin or engage in cognitive dissonance as a way to avoid dealing with it? Why do you think this is the case?

2. What do you most fear if you choose not to hide behind those comfortable old habitual ways of steering clear of these sins?

3. In what ways do you see yourself in the younger son's story in Luke 15:11-32? Which parts of his story don't resonate with your experience?

4. Can you describe a time in your life when you were aware that God was disciplining you? What is the relationship between God's discipline and regret?

Prayer

Father. That name carries pain for so many people.

Father. You know it is colored by some sadness in my life too.

So many have lived harsh alternate versions of the story your Son told to those religious professionals. The idea of returning home to a papa's open arms is the stuff of someone else's happily ever after. Those who've been wounded by an earthly parent whose name was Harsh, Absent, or Abusive may wish to stay far, far away.

I ask for your gift of trust for those who may feel that the distant land is a safer place than in your embrace. Help them to see that you are there waiting for them.

On behalf of those who have tried to hide from you using all manner of evasive maneuvers and have wandered far, I do thank you that the discomfort of your discipline is meant to help us see what you see when you look at our rebel choices. And I thank you that you use those stinging regrets like smelling salts to bring us to our senses so we'll leave the pigpen and come home.

Good and holy Father, I ask these things in the name of your Son, who trusted you without reservation.

Amen.

THREE

DOING A WHOLE LOT OF NOTHING

AVOIDING THE MESSES OF OTHERS

The mistakes I've made are dead to me.
But I can't take back the things I never did.
—Jonathan Safran Foer

The Kitty Genovese syndrome is a nickname for what happens when a whole bunch of people decide to do nothing when doing something is what the situation requires. Kitty was a young woman who was stabbed to death in a densely populated neighborhood in Queens, New York, in 1964. A number of neighbors later reported that they heard her screams but did not call police because they assumed that someone else would do so.

In the end, no one reached out to authorities in time to save her life.

Though later investigations showed that the first reports about the neighbors' passive response to Kitty's screams might have been exaggerated, the case represented the way that individual responsibility sometimes becomes diffused among a group of people so that the buck—and the responsibility—stops nowhere. This has also been called the bystander effect.

If you've ever been in a crowded mall parking lot when a fender bender has occurred and you've thought, "I hope someone calls the police" as you've driven past, you've experienced the bystander effect. We may not feel the pain of "if only" if we put ourselves in the category of bystander, but the Kitty Genovese case reminds us that doing nothing together can leave a heaping helping of regret in its wake.

Of course, there are plenty of times in our lives when there are no bystanders with whom we can share the blame when we choose to do nothing. "Doing nothing" might seem like a perfect way to avoid getting our lives splattered with someone else's messy problems. When we tally our regrets, most of us probably list the things we've done. But we can also accumulate regret by what we haven't done.

Some theologians describe two distinct categories of sin: sins of omission and sins of commission. Yes, sin is sin is sin, all of it an affront to our holy God. But the categories can be helpful when we are considering both our motivations and the effects of our choices. A sin of commission can be described as knowing something is wrong and deciding to do it anyway, such as Adam and Eve eating the fruit from the tree of the knowledge of good and evil (Gen. 3:6) after God had specifically told them not to do so (Gen. 2:16-17).

We commit a sin of omission, on the other hand, when we know God is asking us to do something and we decide not to do it. Maybe it's inconvenient. Maybe it'll cost us something. Maybe we figure someone else will call the police when we hear a young woman screaming. The apostle James underscores that sometimes sin comes in the form of what we haven't done: "If anyone, then, knows the good they ought to do and doesn't do it, it is sin for them" (James 4:17). If I see someone steal an expensive necklace and choose to keep my mouth shut because I don't want the hassle of getting involved in other people's problems, I have sinned by what I haven't done. In effect, the necklace has two thieves: the one who swiped it, and me, the one who saw it happen and didn't report it—or try to stop it.

The Anglican Book of Common Prayer offers a prayer of confession to God that gives us an opportunity to consider the different kinds of ways each one of us sins against him. The categories listed in this prayer also capture the kinds of attitudes and behaviors that leave us with lingering regrets.

Most merciful God, we confess that we have sinned against you in thought, word, and deed, by what we have done, and by what we have left undone. We have not loved you with our whole heart; we have not loved our neighbors as ourselves. We are truly sorry and we humbly repent. For the sake of your Son Jesus Christ, have mercy on us and forgive us; that we may delight in your will, and walk in your ways, to the glory of your name. Amen.

The words that get me every time I've prayed this prayer are "and by what we have left undone." Every single time. God has used those seven little words to show me that my sins of omission may not have led to a place in the Top Ten on my personal "Life's Big Regrets" list, but they have generated plenty of regret nonetheless. If such a list existed, some of my sins of omission are in places number 11 to 20 on that list.

We'll be looking in a later chapter at the unique nature of the regrets we may carry when it comes to the unfinished business we may have with a relative, a friend, or even an enemy and that person dies. But there are plenty of other kinds of "if onlys" we carry when we choose to sit on the sidelines as a spectator when we're being called to engage.

In the 1946 movie classic *It's a Wonderful Life*, small-town banker and real estate developer George Bailey tried to kill himself after his vindictive business nemesis, Mr. Potter, threatened to ruin him. On Christmas Eve, a despairing, drunken George stood on a bridge over a raging river preparing to commit suicide. His guardian angel, Clarence, knew that the only way to steer George from this plan was to tap into George's self-sacrificing character. Clarence threw himself into the river, and George jumped in after him in order to rescue him. As the two men warmed themselves after the episode, George's sense of hopelessness returned.

When George told Clarence it would be better if he'd never been born, Clarence gave George a peek into what the world would have been like without him. One of my favorite moments in this sequence is when George heads to the site of the neighborhood he'd been building the working-class folks of the town. Instead of pretty little cottages he'd built with his clients' dignity in mind, he discovered a neglected old cemetery.

"All I know is this should be Bailey Park," a distraught George told Clarence. "But where are the houses?"

"You weren't here to build them," Clarence replied, then added, "Each man's life touches so many other lives and when he isn't around he leaves an awful hole, doesn't he?"

Seeing vignettes of what life would have been like without him in it awakened George to the richness of the life he had lived. Though he never had the opportunity to follow the dreams of travel and adventure he imagined for himself as a young man, the ethical, kind manner in which he lived in his small town made a difference for everyone around him. George Bailey spent years coveting a different life for himself, but in the daily grind, he put nub to paper and wrote a life full of small but important moral choices that benefitted his family and community.

The Clarence sequence in the movie is a study in the ways our sins of omission can affect those around us. If we opt out of acting when we're given a chance to do so, the effects of our choice not to act often ripple far beyond the moment in ways we simply can't imagine.

In the end, George begged Clarence to give him his old life back. The giddy joy with which he embraced the problems that drove him to the brink of suicide makes me cry every time I've seen the movie. (I estimate that I've seen it at least twenty times.) George discovered that the omission of his presence affected everyone he knew, and he recommitted to being a fully engaged participant in the story of his own wonderful, imperfect life.

On Being There

Our decisions to opt out of responding to the needs to which God calls us are a way of creating an escape clause for ourselves in a nonnegotiable command:

> "The most important one," answered Jesus, "is this: 'Hear, O Israel: The Lord our God, the Lord is one. Love the Lord your God with all your heart and with all your soul and with all your mind and with all your strength.' The second is this: 'Love your neighbor as yourself.' There is no commandment greater than these." (Mark 12:29-31)

Loving God and loving our neighbors isn't convenient. It is apt to splash someone else's mess all over our tidy lives. Jesus told the parable of the Good Samaritan (Luke 10:25-37) to a religious expert looking for a way to avoid the uncomfortable inconvenience of those two foundational commandments. The story Jesus told highlighted the actions of two religious experts who knew very well that God asked them to love him heart, soul, mind, and strength and love their neighbors as they loved themselves. In fact, these leaders in Jesus' story were the kinds of men who had the ancient equivalent of PhDs teaching others about how to do these things in order to honor God.

Yet when they were faced with the mess of a man they each discovered laying on the side of the road, these two respected leaders elected to avert their eyes, reroute their paths, and hustle past him toward their urgent destination, which I believe might have been called Anywhere but Here. The man had been robbed, stripped, beaten, then left for dead. The poor victim's name may as well have been Kitty Genovese.

Jesus contrasted the decision of these two to do nothing with the actions of a man from a group the religious men had deemed as unkosher as a ham sandwich. This member of that outcast Samaritan group stopped beside the wounded man, bandaged his wounds, carried him to safe haven, took care of him, then paid the ancient version of the victim's hospital bill while the man continued to convalesce in safety.

"Which of these three do you think was a neighbor to the man who fell into the hands of robbers?" Jesus asked the loophole-seeker who prompted the story (Luke 10:36). You can almost hear the pin drop two thousand years later.

The man answered Jesus, "The one who had mercy on him" (v. 37). The word Jesus used as the man's answer—"mercy" (*eleos*)—is a word that connotes kindness in action. Kindness in action is a contrast to the stay-out-of-it impulse that we use to convince ourselves that we don't need to get involved, be inconvenienced, or get our sparkling clean clothes dirty with the problems of others. Jesus wasn't impressed with the outfits of those who seemed to have a whole closet of holy wear unstained by tears, dust, sweat, blood, and even a few random mustard stains.

The Blooper Reel

I have a blooper reel of things I chose not to do when I had the power to act. Here are just a few of them:

- I snubbed a new girl in my sixth grade class. I wanted to hang out with my friends and they didn't seem interested in including a new person in our clique.
- I walked past a person picking up scattered groceries in the rain after her sack ripped. I didn't want to get wet.
- I ignored a disabled person wiping down tables at a fast food restaurant who kept trying to say hello to me. I wanted to enjoy my meal without having to make small talk with a stranger.
- I blew off a request from a community group for canned goods for a food drive. I had more important things to do. I can't remember what those things were right now.
- I avoided an elderly relative because she kept repeating the same stories and asking me the same questions. I preferred a more alert conversation partner.

We are presented with pressing needs all day long: homeless people carrying cardboard signs walk between lanes of traffic in search of spare change; emotional commercials featuring sad-eyed puppies pleading with us to adopt them; our mailboxes are packed with solicitations in the mail to feed starving children on the other side of the globe or in our own communities; our own kids ask us to drive them to the mall and by the way, can they have twenty bucks to spend while they're there?

We learn to filter in order to protect ourselves from getting drained dry by those unrelenting requests. We discover how to avert our eyes and keep on walking. We use language like "stewarding our resources" and "maintaining healthy boundaries." And there is biblical wisdom in observing wise boundaries with others:

My son, if you have put up security for your neighbor, if you have shaken hands in pledge for a stranger, you have been trapped by what you said, ensnared by the words of your mouth. So do this, my son, to free yourself, since you have fallen into your neighbor's hands: Go—to the point of exhaustion—and give your neighbor no rest! Allow no sleep to your eyes, no slumber to your eyelids. Free yourself, like a gazelle from the hand of the hunter, like a bird from the snare of the fowler. (Prov. 6:1-5)

Unfortunately, plain old selfishness is sometimes our filter. We have the power to do good and we elect not to do it. Scripture offers us a powerful picture of the kind of regret that comes from silencing the voice of the Spirit and getting in the habit of doing nothing instead.

In Matthew 25:31-46, Jesus tells a story about the way in which at the end of all things he will distinguish between those who've followed him the way sheep follow their shepherd and the "goats" who haven't done so. He measures his followers' faithfulness by the way they responded to those in need and living at the margins of society—the hungry, the thirsty, the stranger, the impoverished, the sick, the prisoner. (Interestingly, his first followers and ambassadors were themselves often the ones at the margins of society! To see what I mean, see Paul's list of the hardships he suffered [2 Cor. 11:23-28].)

Jesus celebrates the actions of the sheep that acted according to his character, "Whatever you did for one of the least of these brothers and sisters of mine, you did for me" (Matt. 25:40).

He then pronounces judgment on the goats for not acting. "For I was hungry and you gave me nothing to eat, I was thirsty and you gave me nothing to drink, I was a stranger and you did not invite me in, I needed clothes and you did not clothe me, I was sick and in prison and you did not look after me" (vv. 42-43).

The goats' plaintive response to this question is soaked in "if only." "Lord, when did we see you hungry or thirsty or a stranger or needing clothes or sick or in prison, and did not help you?" (v. 44).

There is no hard-and-fast rule that can help us sort the needs presented to us into tidy categories: this one is a boundary-crosser, that one is an honest sheep-style bleat for help to which I should respond. And maybe that's the point. When we seek to follow our Good Shepherd, that active pursuit leads us to inquire and respond (kindness in action!) to needs very differently than we will if we bless ourselves to call all the shots.

Doing Nothing: The Upgraded Version

It is possible to accumulate regret by doing a little more than nothing. We may decide to act . . . sort of. When we do less than what is really needed in a particular situation, we are choosing an upgraded version of a sin of omission.

I like to think of myself as a loyal and honest friend. But that super-friend self-image I have of myself is challenged by the neglectful way I've treated a few lonely, hurting people who have entered my life in search of help and companionship.

My friendship with a woman named Jennifer is a perfect example of this. My family had just begun attending the church where Jennifer served on staff. She had a big personality and limitless energy. We hit it off right away. As time went on, I discovered that lurking underneath that high-octane public persona was a great deal of brokenness she kept in the shadows, just out of view of most of the congregation. This brokenness included an active eating disorder, a failing marriage, and intense discord with her three teens.

I was a sympathetic listener, and soon Jennifer was calling me a couple of times a day, sometimes to shoot the breeze, other times to pour out her heart. At first, I was honored she'd chosen to confide in me, but I realized after a few months of this that I'd gradually allowed this relationship to cross wise boundaries. The relationship was a one-way street.

My job was to listen empathetically to Jennifer for hours every week. In turn, I was supposed to remain silent about my own life, as she rarely asked about anything happening to me. She invariably changed the subject back to herself when she did inquire how I was doing.

All my listening wasn't really helping her. While Jennifer sought my advice about her seemingly intractable problems, she had an endless list of reasons why she couldn't seek help for her troubled marriage and addiction or share her struggles with anyone else at church. Jennifer really didn't want to change.

My growing resentment over the time-suck of the relationship forced me to consider why I'd allowed it to consume my time like kudzu. It was meeting my icky need to be needed in a way that wasn't redemptive for either Jennifer or me. I didn't know how to untangle myself from the unhealthy aspects of the relationship gracefully, so I did it poorly instead by not confronting her.

I ducked her phone calls and generally made myself less available to her. I may have had to choose those actions anyway, but without speaking to her frankly about my growing frustrations or attempting to renegotiate the relationship, I now recognize that I was no better of a friend to her than she'd been to me.

Our relationship faded as I engaged in a systematic campaign of avoiding her. She eventually left the church, then relocated. Our family then moved out of the area a couple of years later.

Though I initially felt relief after I downshifted my relationship with Jennifer from fourth gear to neutral, once those feelings faded, I realized I hadn't acted with the kind of courageous, sheep-like, Shepherd-honoring integrity in the way I handled those crossed boundaries.

The regret I felt about my relationship with Jennifer showed me that there are countless ways to do less than what God asks of us—which isn't all that different from doing nothing at all.

Regret that accompanies a sin of omission may tease us into trying to fill in the blanks of what might have happened if only we'd acted instead of sitting on the sidelines. That tease is false advertising trying to get us to buy something that isn't real. The real is found when we allow our regrets about what we haven't done to help us recognize our divided hearts and our need to be carried, like the wounded man bleeding on the side of the road, to a place where we can be restored.

Reflection Questions

1. Can you recall a time in your life when you've experienced the bystander effect? What were your reasons at the time for choosing not to act?

2. Have you ever been on the receiving end of the actions of a Good Samaritan? What did the experience show you about the nature of mercy, of kindness in action?

3. When or with whom are boundaries most necessary in your life? Why?

4. When have you chosen to do less than what God may have been asking you to do? How would you describe your reasons behind this decision?

Prayer

Merciful Shepherd, I have waited for someone else to make the call. I have walked past a person you've asked me to help because I did not want to soil my pretty outfit or rearrange my precious schedule. I have used the notion of boundaries as my excuse not to act when I should have been learning obedience to you.

I have left things undone that you asked me to do. I ask your Holy Spirit to search my heart and bring to mind the things I've left undone—or underdone. I have not loved you wholeheartedly. I have loved myself in the wrong ways, and I have not loved others well as a result.

Lord, transform the regret I feel over my inaction into a change of direction. Thank you for your kindness in action toward me. Thank you for your mercy.

I pray these things in the name of the One who chose to act on my behalf by coming into this messy world to carry me to safety.

Amen.

FOUR

I WANT WHAT I HAVE AND I WANT WHAT YOU HAVE TOO

STEALING YOUR OWN LIFE

> I didn't know you could steal your own life. And I didn't
> know that it would bring you no more benefit than
> about anything else you might steal.
>
> —Cormac McCarthy

• •

The foursquare farmhouse was perfumed with the scent of roasting turkey when the final branch of extended family spilled into the house via the back door. Hugs and laughter rose to greet them as towel-wrapped casserole dishes were transferred from arms to cluttered countertops. The children ran to join the rest of the cousins who were in the front room playing board games. The older teens joined the group in the den watching the football game. Correction: the game was on, but the congenial group was telling family stories and trading news. Five or six women were clustered in the kitchen, putting the final touches on the most anticipated meal of the year.

Just as he did every year about a half an hour before Thanksgiving dinner was going to be served, Grandpa entered the controlled chaos of the kitchen to sharpen the old carving knife. While this solemn ceremony was taking place, some of the aunts began carrying a Macy's Thanksgiving Day Parade of platters and bowls of homemade side dishes to the large dining room. There was a long oak dining table with every leaf inserted, surrounded by a friendly mismatch of chairs including an aging high chair, and two card tables pushed together for the younger set.

As most of the pre-meal frenzy abated, Grandma called. "OK, everyone, time to eat!" On cue, the groups scattered throughout the house converged in the dining room and assembled themselves in noisy chaos around the tables.

"Let's pray," Grandpa called out. A hush fell over the room. "Dear Lord, we thank you for the bounty around this table, for all the ways you have provided for our family this year. Thank you for bringing Cousin Frank through his bypass surgery, and for the gift of our newest grandbaby. We thank you most of all for the gift of your Son, who offers each of us abundant and eternal life with you."

He then launched into the doxology. Every voice in the room blended into a perfect four-part harmony, "Praise God from whom all blessings flow . . ."

My Real Deal Thanksgiving Meal

My mom's voice cut through my Thanksgiving daydream like an electric carving knife. "Hey, Michelle. Get downstairs. It's time to eat."

I'd been bunkered in my bedroom for much of the afternoon, imagining everyone else except me was enjoying a Norman Rockwell holiday. I walked down the stairs, where the football game blared. The sound of the crowd made it feel as though there were more people than just my mom, dad, sister, and me in the house.

My mom cooked only once a year, and today was it: green bean casserole, canned sweet potatoes mashed with pineapple and topped with giant puffy marshmallows, packaged bread stuffing, a can of jellied cranberry sauce dumped onto a glass plate and then sliced into rounds with the raw edge of the can lid, and turkey, of course. My mom proclaimed, "Thanksgiving is my favorite holiday." It was as close to the giving of thanks as our family got.

Though there was plenty of food for the four of us, I was hungry for something more. I wanted to be with that family in the farmhouse, surrounded by twenty-three happy, loving relatives. I wished it so much I could almost taste my fantasy grandma's flaky-crust homemade pumpkin pie.

Disorienting Our Soul

Some of us wish for fancy, camera-ready homes. Some obsess about how to obtain a smaller waistline and the wardrobe to show it off. Others yearn for power or more money or a different spouse.

The Bible names this desire coveting. The prohibition against coveting is the last of the Ten Commandments: "You shall not covet your neighbor's house. You shall not covet your neighbor's wife, or his male or female servant, his ox or donkey, or anything that belongs to your neighbor" (Exod. 20:17). The invisible asterisk on this list includes, among other things, my imaginary family Thanksgiving. I coveted the kind of family I saw in Norman Rockwell paintings and on TV shows like *The Waltons*. I missed what God had given me because I was constantly staring at the lush green grass on the other side of the proverbial fence.

Coveting is the yearning to possess something that isn't ours to have. Envy is the name of that miserable discontent that accompanies that yearning. Coveting disorients our souls away from the gifts God has given us and the relationship he wants with us. Author William Barclay noted, "Covetousness is . . . a sin with a very wide range. If it is the desire for money, it leads to theft. If it is the desire for prestige, it leads to evil ambition. If it is the desire for power, it leads to sadistic tyranny. If it is the desire for a person, it leads to sexual sin."[1]

No matter in what area of life it manifests, covetousness leaves a trail of regret-worthy actions and attitudes in its wake. When we throw aside what belongs to us in order to gain what belongs to someone else, "if only" is the result.

When Having It All Isn't Enough

Years of being on the run from King Saul, the man he would eventually succeed, had shaped a carefree shepherd boy into a man who knew who he was and who his God was. That connection tethered David within the boundaries of the Law. It freed him to respond with speed and wisdom to one daunting challenge after another.

David's lengthy, difficult, and unorthodox job training program ended with the death of Saul. David stepped into the role of king for which he'd been anointed when he was a lad. Though he faced a few military skirmishes with neighboring nations as he had to repair the chaos his predecessor left in his wake, David enjoyed the favor of the people and of God.

Things were going so well, in fact, that he could relax and delegate some of his leadership responsibilities to others: "In the spring, at the time when kings go off to war, David sent Joab out with the king's men and the whole Israelite army. They destroyed the Ammonites and besieged Rabbah. But David remained in Jerusalem" (2 Sam. 11:1).

David felt confident enough in his military leaders to stay behind. This was a relatively unusual decision in those days. Most leaders accompanied their troops to the front lines in those days.

But David had it all.

Well, almost all.

One evening, he headed to his rooftop, perhaps to catch a cool breeze or to survey his kingdom. From this vantage point, he saw something that didn't belong to him.

More precisely, he saw *someone* who didn't belong to him. Her name was Bathsheba, also known as Mrs. Uriah the Hittite. She was up on her own rooftop, bathing after her monthly period ended, following the Law's dictates (Lev. 15:19-24). Though 1950s Hollywood movies portrayed Bathsheba in this moment as a flirty and promiscuous woman, in reality, she was simply obeying the Law in the way other women of her time did.

She responded in obedience, too, when she received a summons from a messenger at the palace, commanding her to present herself before King David. A king's subject didn't question a command. She obeyed.

The Bible gives us the headlines of what happened next: "She came to him, and he slept with her" (2 Sam. 11:4). David coveted her, and he took what didn't belong to him.

Weeks later, Bathsheba sent word to David. She was pregnant, and he was the only one who could be the father. Her husband, Uriah, had been gone for weeks, serving with the other men David had sent out on military duty.

In order to cover his tracks, David summoned Uriah back to Jerusalem, had a chitchatty meeting with him, then proceeded to give Uriah the night off from his duty. David was hoping that Uriah would go home and make love to his wife that night. He was banking on Bathsheba's silence. Who would believe her anyway? If he said he wasn't the baby's father, who was going to argue with him? He was the king, and no one argued with the king.

Uriah understood obedience too. While he was on duty serving the king, he'd vowed to be single-minded about his obligation. Uriah didn't go home to his wife, choosing instead to sleep at the gate of the palace with the other servants.

The next day, David asked Uriah why he didn't spend the night with Bathsheba. Uriah replied, "The ark and Israel and Judah are staying in tents, and my commander Joab and my lord's men are camped in the open country. How could I go to my house to eat and drink and make love to my wife? As surely as you live, I will not do such a thing!" (2 Sam. 11:11).

David resorted to Plan B. He invited Uriah to hang at the palace with him for a couple of days, wining and dining it up. David got him a little drunk, but his tipsy state didn't erode Uriah's sense of duty. Each evening, Uriah headed to the gate to sleep instead of going home to Bathsheba.

Plan C

This man who was innocently doing the right thing was getting in the way of David's sin. David needed a foolproof Plan C. He sent faithful, obedient Uriah to his death in battle. David appeared to be the perfect gentleman leader, sending a consoling note to Uriah's commander and bringing the pregnant widow, Bathsheba, into his home to be one of his wives. It looked like David's coveting got him exactly what he wanted. It appeared he'd gotten away with it, scot-free. Not a single "if only" in sight.

Until he got caught.

His sin was called out by Nathan, a prophet sent by God. To David's great credit, instead of bemoaning or excusing his string of terrible moral choices, in the face of the burning light of God's exposure, he went straight to regret. He told Nathan, "I have sinned against the Lord" (2 Sam. 12:13).

Nathan delivered a message of God's judgment, telling David that God forgave his sin and would continue to give him life. Before David had a chance to exhale, Nathan added, "But because by doing this you have shown utter contempt for the LORD, the son born to you will die" (v. 14). That very day, the little baby was struck gravely ill. A single word from his Creator brought the child to the brink of death.

I can imagine Bathsheba walking the ill baby back and forth across the floor for hours on end. The sound of her anguished pleas for God's help, perhaps even pleading that he take her life instead of her innocent child, mingled with the sound of the baby's labored breath.

David went to war on behalf of his son, and, I believe, on his own behalf as well. He donned the clothing of a mourner, refused to eat, and splayed his body on the floor, begging God to save the life of this innocent child. His remorseful display of grief and repentance continued for a week straight.

When the baby died, David's staff was afraid to tell him. Their fearless leader had become a weeping, inconsolable puddle on the floor. The shift in their behavior as they murmured in the hallways just beyond his earshot triggered the question from David: "Is the child dead?" (v. 19).

Someone answered in the affirmative, and then the staff ducked, waiting for the emotional breakdown they'd been expecting for a week.

Instead, David rose, got dressed, went to worship God, then returned to his palace and ate a full meal. His attendants couldn't believe what they were seeing. When they asked him about it, his response startled them, to say the least.

He explained the release: "While the child was still alive, I fasted and wept. I thought, 'Who knows? The LORD may be gracious to me and let the child live.' But now that he is dead, why should I go on fasting? Can I bring him back again? I will go to him, but he will not return to me" (vv. 22-23).

My mind understands the logic that David's moral failure was going to make him a bitter punch line to his people and would make a weakened Israel a potential target of the surrounding nations. But even with that understanding, my soul has questions. I'll confess I don't understand why the mother and baby had to suffer when it was his daddy who'd sinned and sinned some more. I do want to take a moment to honor this little boy, as he did the most difficult work imaginable in a very short time. This baby pointed his powerful father back toward God with every labored breath of his short life, and he saved many other lives in the process.

David's pile-on of sins began with one. William Penn said, "Covetousness is the greatest of monsters, as well as the root of all evil." I believe David would have agreed with him. Covetousness tells us no matter what we have, it's never enough.

The Work of "If Only"

I know a young woman who obsessed about having a different life through her teens; specifically, the looks, money, relaxed house rules, and abundant male attention she believed a particular friend of hers possessed. She alternated between copying her friend and raging at her family for not giving her everything she thought her friend had. The process of forging an identity for herself during her teen years and learning who God made her to be was short-circuited by envy and coveting. In effect, she wore a mask with her friend's face on it, hoping the world would believe her imitation of her friend was the truth about her.

The consequences of trying to be someone she wasn't piled up throughout her twenties and into her early thirties until "if only" slowly began to pierce her mask. What had she lost in pursuit of a fantasy existence that never fit her because it never belonged to her to begin with?

Author C. S. Lewis said,

It would seem that Our Lord finds our desires not too strong, but too weak. We are half-hearted creatures, fooling about with drink and sex and ambition when infinite joy is offered us, like an ignorant child who wants to go on making mud pies in a slum because he cannot imagine what is meant by the offer of a holiday at the sea. We are far too easily pleased.[2]

The sin of coveting divides our hearts and causes us to pursue lesser things, stealing from ourselves in order to do so. Our regrets, then, may serve as an alarm system, alerting us to the fact that something is missing from our lives, and that something might just be us.

Reflection Questions

1. In what areas of your life do you imagine that the "greener grass" of someone else's life is far better than what God has given you?

2. Have you ever witnessed someone in a position of power, or someone who seems to have it all, acting on the envy that comes from coveting something they don't possess? What does this tell you about the nature of coveting?

3. When you consider a regret you've been carrying for a long time, can you trace it back to its birth? What was it that you coveted back then? How do you view the object of that long-ago desire today?

4. Where might coveting as a cause and regret as an effect be closely linked in your life?

Prayer

O God, your Word says, "Every good and perfect gift is from above, coming down from the Father of the heavenly lights, who does not change like shifting shadows" (James 1:17). Instead of receiving like a trusting child what you place in my hands, I look around me at what the other kids are getting. I want what I have and I want what I think they have too.

The wanting is so powerful sometimes, Jesus. And it leads me to find ways to satiate that desire. Even if I get what I think I want, what I had to do to get it leaves me with a case of regret. My sin of coveting obscures my view of you.

I have a tendency to list my regrets instead of naming my sins when I talk to you about these matters. I tell you I regret that I wished away Thanksgiving instead of acknowledging to you that my coveting blinded me to what you had given me. So many of my regrets have been birthed out of my pale desires for things that can never satisfy all the longings of my divided heart.

Help me to say the words that David said to you: I have sinned against you and you only. I am at once unworthy and ravenous to receive your forgiveness.

Yet you generously offer it to me through the gift of your Son, Jesus.

Thank you.

FIVE

HIDING IN A STACK OF FIG LEAVES

WHEN SOMEONE ELSE'S SIN TRIES TO WRITE YOUR STORY

*Regret is . . . an unavoidable result of any loss,
for in loss we lose the tomorrow that we needed
to make right our yesterday or today.*

—Jerry Sittser

You've won a week at a luxury resort. Part of your prize package is three meals a day prepared just for you by a famous chef. She'll cook you anything your heart desires. So you order ramen with a side order of canned fruit cocktail at every meal, hold those nasty maraschino cherries.

When we become a victim of someone else's sin, the effects of that person's lousy choices may limit our ability to consider making a healthy choice for ourselves. We can't imagine that anything other than ramen and canned fruit cocktail might be an option for us.

While our coveting habits may contribute to our list of regrets, they are not the only thing that creates an "if only" in our lives. If we've experienced trauma or abuse, particularly during childhood or adolescence, we may create unrealistic boundaries around our lives in order to protect ourselves from additional hurt. Those boundaries keep us ordering ramen when we could have had a gorgeous gourmet feast.

There are some trauma victims who are gifted with a great deal of inner resilience that helps them abound in the aftermath of their trauma as survivors. A couple of real-life examples illustrate this: As a result of his participation in a bombing campaign against his country's unjust government, Nelson Mandela spent twenty-seven years in prison. He emerged to become president of his nation, leading South Africa to an end of its official policy of apartheid. Corrie ten Boom lost her entire family in the prisons and concentration camps of the Nazis as a result of their choice to shelter Jews in a hiding place in their home in the Netherlands. After her release from Ravensbrück at the end of the war, ten Boom had a long and fruitful ministry sharing her stories of God's love and mercy.

We know of these examples because they are exceptions. Most of us who've experienced trauma or abuse at the selfish, sinful hands of others are left with lingering effects. When we are victimized, we are changed. The way we view the world, our diminished ability to trust others and God, and our core sense of self are changed too. How we long to have—or begin living—a "normal" life. However, ignoring or minimizing this pain means we may stick to a diet of ramen and fruit cocktail because it is the only choice we believe is available to us.

At some point, when "if only" kicks in, we may realize as my friend Kate did that our limited diet meant we've missed out on a feast.

The Good Girl Way

"This has to be our secret, Katie, or else something terrible will happen to your family and it will be all your fault."

When her teenage babysitter sexually abused seven-year-old Kate, these were the words he always said to her. Jason always said them with such tenderness that it made it sound as though he were on her side, helping her fight for her family.

She had to keep the secret to keep her family safe, so she let her brain float like a red balloon on a long string during Jason's close encounters of the worst kind. Disconnecting her head from her body was the only way Kate could protect her family from that Terrible Thing that might happen to them if she ever told what was happening to her.

If she disconnected from what was happening to her, then she couldn't accidentally let slip the secret. Her parents seemed to like Jason and often commented how responsible and respectful he was. "We really like having a male babysitter who likes to play with your little brother," her mom said on more than once occasion.

Even though Jason was the babysitter, she believed it was her job to do everything she could to keep her little brother safe, so she let herself float far, far away whenever Jason came into her room to play his secret game. She prayed with a child's faith that the time he spent in her room would be enough to keep him away from her brother.

Eventually, Jason got an after-school job and no longer baby-sat for the family. Kate buried the unexposed memories of Jason's sexual abuse deep in her long-term storage and built a G-rated, good-girl life on top of that foundation. In high school, she prayed a prayer of commitment, surrendering her life to Christ and asking him to forgive all of her sins.

Whenever she prayed after that, she grocery-listed every wrong thing she'd ever done while wishing that the words of forgiveness she'd heard from sermons and hymns would be her experience too. But she never felt washed clean, whiter than snow, free, restored, or whole. When she questioned a well-meaning youth pastor about why she felt guilty no matter how many times she confessed her sins, he told her she needed to have faith that Christ had forgiven her and simply ignore her feelings. In the process, she learned to silence her experience and mute her talents, gifts, and dreams.

Though his words were theologically correct, the unprocessed abuse in the young woman's life formed a filter of shame that warped the truth into its own image. Hyperresponsible Kate had learned as a child how to ignore her feelings. It meant church gave her the labels she could apply to her life. She would be a good girl in the name of Christ.

Guilt and Shame Are Not the Same

Because guilt and shame are so closely connected, we often use the two words interchangeably. If we understand the difference between the two, it can change the way we understand how regret is birthed in our lives, awaken us to the kinds of guilt and shame that can serve a redemptive purpose, and equip us to confront the kinds of guilt and shame that imprison us.

There is a difference:

"Guilt" = I did something bad.

"Shame" = I am bad.

"Guilt" is a judicial term. It means I have broken a law or committed a crime. It doesn't have anything to do with how I might feel about my crime. We are guilty before God—and often, against others, when we sin. When Adam and Eve ate of the forbidden fruit in the garden of Eden (Gen. 3:1-6), they did something bad. They were guilty.

Shame, on the other hand, is a statement of how we perceive ourselves, how we feel, and how we believe others view or relate to us. The feelings of discomfort, misery, and/or embarrassment isolate us from others. When Adam and Eve grabbed fig leaves to cover themselves in the wake of their forbidden fruit feast (Gen. 3:7), their impromptu fashion show happened as a result of the shame they felt in the wake of the guilt they incurred.

Guilt and shame can serve a corrective purpose in our lives, alerting us to the reality that we are out of good relationship with God and others. Or it can trap us in a sinkhole-pocked swamp of regret. In her book I Thought It Was Just Me (But It Isn't), Dr. Brené Brown explains the difference:

> If I experience shame because I lose patience with my child and I blame myself for being a bad mother, I'm more likely to be pulled even farther into my shame. If, on the other hand, I lose patience with my child, experience shame, then hold myself accountable for my behavior, I'm more likely to apologize to my child and figure out how to move through the shame so I can be the parent I want to be.[1]

The kind of shame that leads us to label ourselves as lousy wives or mothers—or ugly or stupid or klutzy or undeserving of mercy or any of the lies we then use to create our identity—is nothing more than a stack of artfully arranged fig leaves.

Shame keeps us in hiding.

There are lots of ways to hide. We may act out. We may smother our pain in addiction. As Kate discovered, performance in the form of "a good Christian life" is one of those hiding places that's right out there in plain sight.

Kate was a sweet, helpful, friendly girl; she'd worked hard to become a model Christian as a way to cover her deep sense of shame. She headed to college and married Tim, the charming spiritual superstar of her campus fellowship group, two weeks after the pair graduated.

Not long after they returned from their honeymoon, she discovered by clicking on an innocent-looking link her husband left open on his computer that he had a porn habit. With tears and promises, he confessed and promised he'd never, ever, ever look at the stuff again. Ever.

It was a promise he would break dozens of times over the next two years. Tim tried various remedies to cauterize his addiction once and for all—fasting, accountability software, a support group—but none of them lasted for more than a few weeks at best.

Kate blamed herself almost entirely for Tim's addiction. If only she were prettier. If only she were sexier. If only she were a better wife. If only she could figure out where the secret "if only" switch was hidden in this mess, she'd be able to flip it to the "off" position and save her crumbling marriage.

High-Performing Shame

In chapter 2, we looked at the story of the younger son in Jesus' parable of the prodigal son, found in Luke 15:11-32. Oh, how we love that story of the father's lavish welcome home for his younger son. If you recall, the young man demanded his future inheritance right this moment, then left home and blew the entire sum on prostitutes and partying.

But there is another son in the story. The father's older son had always done everything he was supposed to do. Always. When the older brother realized that his good-for-nothing younger brother was being received from his long trip to a distant land as though he were a returning war hero, his fury at the news unmasked a lifetime of carefully managed shame. He fled from the scene of his younger brother's party. When his father pursued him, he decanted these sour words:

But he answered his father, "Look! All these years I've been slaving for you and never disobeyed your orders. Yet you never gave me even a young goat so I could celebrate with my friends. But when this son of yours who has squandered your property with prostitutes comes home, you kill the fattened calf for him!" (Luke 15:29-30)

Jesus was speaking to the religious authorities of his day, people who'd prided themselves on following all the rules; they'd long forgotten those rules were meant to make them a light to the "younger son" nations around them. The older son is like those of us who cover our shame in performance and hyper-precise obedience. The older son appears to believe that his performance is what gives him value. Scratch just below the surface of his heated words and you will find someone who believes love has to be earned. Scratch a little deeper, and you'll find someone who can never be secure that he's ever really done enough to deserve that love.

In light of the fact that in the parable the father is a good papa, it is worth noting that it isn't always the biggies of trauma or abuse that leave shame in their wake. Sometimes a single, well-aimed sentence or painful experience can leave shame festering in the fissures of each one of our hearts, no matter how happy our home or idyllic our childhood.

"Some of us . . . take a lifelong lease on shame; it is our permanent home," writes Dr. Louis Smedes in his classic work, *Shame and Grace: Healing the Shame We Don't Deserve.* He writes, "We are not prodigal sons who might come to our senses if we felt a shock of acute shame; we are the obedient sons who stay at home and still suffer the constant cramps of chronic shame."[2]

This is not the kind of remorseful shame that alerts us to the presence of sin in our lives. It doesn't lead us to God's redemption and healing. It is the kind of shame that leads us to think and act in ways that generate regret. This older son's shame led to a life marked by fear (I must be good or I won't be loved) and comparison (My brother is valued more than I am). It is the kind of shame that obscured the older son's ability to fully live into the relationship his father was offering him.

When I read the parable of the prodigal, I see evidence that the older son in the story has a well-defended place of shame in his heart. The older son may not have ever colored outside the "good boy" lines, but his explosion of anger toward his father (Luke 15:28) is an expression of regret about all the energy he's expended in legalistic performance.

His father's response to him is our Father's response to each one of us who might be hiding in shame. Just as the father in the parable ordered a new cloak to clothe the slave-stink of his pig-scented younger son when he returned home, he covers his older son's shame in love and dignity with these incredible words: "My son, . . . you are always with me, and everything I have is yours" (v. 31).

Peeling Away the Layers

Kate had lived her life behind the mask of the good girl until she and Tim found themselves in a marriage counselor's office. The counselor suggested a few individual sessions with each one of them. When it was Kate's turn with the counselor, she carefully explained in her best Christianese how her husband's choices were 92 percent her responsibility.

The counselor recognized Kate's misplaced sense of responsibility was protecting something deeper inside of her. Over the next few weeks, the counselor's gentle, probing questions peeled away Kate's layers of emotional fig leaves protecting the well-buried source of so much of her shame: the abuse she'd experienced as a child.

When Jason violated seven-year-old Kate, then told her it was her job to keep her family safe by keeping the abuse a secret, she learned to diminish her own value, ignore her own perceptions, and submerge her emotions underneath the warped version of responsibility her babysitter presented to her. That shame left her disconnected from God's love and her own identity. Though she appeared to be living a holy life, her good-girl ways were in large part a self-protective shield.

Though she had no clue before the wedding that her husband had a porn addiction, her overripe sense of responsibility was a sad-but-perfect match for her husband's habits. Her well-established sense of shame convinced her that she had to protect him with her performance-oriented behavior too.

"Who is protecting you, Kate?" the counselor asked.

Kate couldn't answer the question. But her tears of anger peeled away the final protective layer hiding the abuse she'd suffered.

If you've experienced abuse or other forms of trauma, please know that it was not your fault, no matter what you've been told to the contrary.

I'll repeat it again: It was not your fault.

You may find that some time with a trained counselor can help you peel back the fig leaves. See the appendix for some suggestions on how you might find a capable counselor.

God used her counselor to help Kate recognize that the abuse was not her fault and see how shame masquerading as moral guilt had defined and limited her. Kate began to feel something she'd never before experienced. She felt a deep sense of regret. She'd missed so much in her life because of what had been done to her when she was seven years old. Who might she have been if Jason had been caught and she'd gotten help—better yet, if Jason had never been her babysitter in the first place? If only . . .

Kate's ability to engage honestly in healthy relationships with God and with others, including her husband, who had shame issues of his own to deal with, had been buried under a small mountain of carefully positioned fig leaves. Regret is never, ever meant to be a destination in our lives.

Kate's regrets became the vehicle that helped her identify what was waiting for her beyond the artificial "good girl" boundaries she'd constructed for herself. As she prayerfully faced those regrets, she was able for the first time in her life to prayerfully begin to discover the abundant life God had for her on the other side of those old boundaries of hers.

Reflection Questions

1. If you've been a victim of trauma or abuse, do you have a sense that the experience has created boundaries in your life that may not otherwise need to be there? How so?

2. How have guilt and/or shame served a training purpose in your life?

3. If a sense of personal shame has dictated some of the earlier decisions you've made in your life, what story might your regrets about those decisions be telling you?

4. What prayer would you offer in response to the words the father in the parable said to his older son ("everything I have is yours")?

Prayer

"If I sinned, you would be watching me and would not let my offense go unpunished. If I am guilty—woe to me! Even if I am innocent, I cannot lift my head, for I am full of shame and drowned in my affliction" (Job 10:14-15).

Holy One, I acknowledge my guilt before you. I have sinned against you in many ways and recognize that my remorse over these things is meant to carry me back to you.

I also recognize that some of the shame I've carried has caused me to carry responsibility for things or people never, ever intended for me. As a result, there are times when I have been like the older son in the story you told, Jesus. My anger at the injustice of it all is a parting of the fig leaves I've used to cover that shame.

There have been other times in my life when that shame has made my decisions for me. Time has passed—too much time!—as I've lived within the false limits of that shame. And now I feel the discomfort of regret about the things I've elected not to do, to try, or to be.

What am I to do with that discomfort, Lord? How am I to respond to these regrets? Could it be that they are here to move me from this place?

I don't know.

Father, I wait here, stripped of some of my fig leaves by these uncomfortable questions and pray that you will come to me and cover me in the way the father in the story did, sheltering both older and younger son with his love.

Amen.

SIX

WHAT'S IN THE VAULT?
COMPARTMENTALIZING AS A WAY TO SILENCE THE PAST

My dad used to say that living with regrets was like
driving a car that only moved in reverse.

—Jodi Picoult

- -

I was pleased to see Deanna's number pop up on my caller I.D. We hadn't chatted in a while.

I imagined we were going to do a little catching up. "How are you?"

She skipped the small talk. "Well, things are kind of rough here."

I knew her life was overflowing with stress. She was busy working two part-time jobs in order to make ends meet in her household. Her husband's construction business had failed a couple of years earlier. Her widowed mother was in failing health. It was a script for a crisis. I waited for her to continue. The moments ticked by.

"Deanna . . . are you still there?" I wasn't sure what to expect from my steady, solid, responsible friend, but it certainly wasn't her response.

"I wish my life were over."

I buzzed through my mental files, racing to come up with the right response. The National Institute of Mental Health estimates that nearly 10 percent of the U.S. population is battling a serious mood disorder in any given year. This figure includes those who suffer from bipolar disorder as well as clinical depression. Suicide talk is never, ever anything to ignore or minimize. I asked her if she was considering taking her own life.

"Yeah, I've been tempted to end my life, but I think I'm too big of a coward to actually go through with it. Plus, I couldn't do that to my kids." Her voice trailed off. She sounded so tired.

I told her how much I admired her courage for reaching out to me when it must have taken every last drop of her emotional energy to do so. She said a few days earlier she'd learned that her husband's "recreational" gambling habit had contributed to his business failure. In addition, her oldest daughter had been arrested over the weekend for marijuana possession. "There is so much pain in this household, and it seems as though there's no way out."

Deanna repeated several times in the course of our conversation that she deserved every bit of this woe. She was finally getting what was coming to her. She was playing the role of all three of Job's "comforters" while simultaneously living out her own Job-like experiences.

How could she deserve her daughter's partying? Her mother's failing health? Her husband's gambling addiction? Before we ended the call, Deanna assured me she would be seeking help for her deep depression, and she promised to call me or someone else she trusted in her life if the suicidal thoughts became more insistent.

Throughout the next few days, I checked in with her regularly. I was glad to learn she'd followed through with her promise to seek out professional help. I wanted her to know I'd been praying for her constantly and was on her support team. But every time I did, I kept thinking about those haunting words of regret she'd voiced during our first phone call. A few days later, I asked her as gently as I could why she thought she deserved all the hard stuff that was happening in her life.

"If you knew what I've done, you wouldn't be asking that question," Deanna replied.

I'd known her for more than two decades. I couldn't possibly imagine what terrible secret this conservative, shy woman could be hiding, and I told her so.

Sniffles turned to sobs as she willed herself to say the words: "I had an abortion during freshman year in college." She'd never told anyone, including her husband. Meanwhile, she'd gotten very good at compartmentalizing things. Family and friends in one compartment, work in another, God in another. And the abortion locked safely away, buried in a vault in a distant, neglected corner of her heart.

"Every single problem in my life can be traced to that decision." Her tears had slowed, and weariness registered in her voice. "I can accept God's forgiveness for almost everything else in my life except that. How could he forgive me for what I did to my baby?"

I knew all too well the way that regret hisses at us, telling us that our particular sin is the one that crossed the line and found the end of God's mercy.

And I also knew Jesus didn't carry a list of exemptions when he headed to the cross.

Kintsugi

Deanna's secret was one factor contributing to her depression, but it certainly wasn't the only factor. She acknowledged that she was suffering through especially difficult midlife physiological and hormonal changes in addition to her complicated list of relational and emotional stressors.

As it turned out, Deanna's despair was a turning point in her life. Her crisis was a plea for a restored life and a reunited heart. The prayer, medical care, and emotional support she received in the months following her desperate phone call to me reflected God's *kintsugi* process through which he restores our souls when we are broken and hurting: "The LORD is close to the brokenhearted and saves those who are crushed in spirit" (Ps. 34:18).

Japanese potters developed the kintsugi repair technique where they use a compound that includes molten gold to rejoin the broken clay pieces. The repaired pieces are made useful once again, and often become lovelier than they were in their original form. Kintsugi is a wonderful picture of the way God restores broken hearts. He doesn't erase the evidence or memory of heartbreak. Instead, he makes it beautiful and repurposes us for new uses.

A divided heart, on the other hand, creates a different spiritual dynamic. A divided heart conjures images of two-faced hypocrites who charm authority figures or people who can advance their cause while treating those who don't serve their purposes like trash. If you've ever seen an episode of the 1950s sitcom *Leave It to Beaver*, you may remember the Eddie Haskell character garnered most of his laugh track laughs from his well-played hypocrisy.

The playacting of the hypocrite drew some of Jesus' most biting words. He often challenged the religious people of his day for the wreckage their divided hearts caused in the lives of others. Matthew 23 provides one extended example of this, but it certainly isn't the only one.

However, a divided heart can be a little harder to detect. Deanna was a forthright, gentle, and thoughtful woman. "Hypocrite" wouldn't have been a word anyone would have ever chosen to describe her. Yet a division in her heart caused by her regret protected the vault in which she kept the secret of her abortion.

Nineteenth-century preacher Charles Spurgeon spoke about how a divided heart affects our lives:

A stony heart may be turned to flesh but turn a divided heart into whatsoever you please, so long as it is divided, all is ill. Nothing can go right when that which should be one organ becomes two; when the one motive power begins to send forth its life-floods into two diverse channels, and so creates intestine strife and war. A united heart is life to a man, but if the heart be cut in twain, in the highest, deepest, and most spiritual sense, he dies. It is a disease which is not only affecting a vital part, but affecting it after the most deadly fashion.[1]

The antidote for a divided heart is found in King David's prayer: "Give me an undivided heart, that I may fear your name" (Ps. 86:11). Uniting entails surrendering to the process by which God reconnects those divided parts of our being. He alone can make us whole.

Rarely is this process of gaining a united heart met without resistance.

Satan has a stake in the game. A divided heart gives him a comfortable stage from which to stand and fire allegations at us. Revelation 12:10 describes the unrelenting nature of his critical activity: "The accuser of our brothers and sisters, who accuses them before our God day and night."

Deanna knew that regret can take on the personality of an unrelenting prosecuting attorney. For years, that voice told her she was a murderer.

Our Defender

Three of the Gospels record the story of a man possessed by demons who lived naked among the tombs outside his town (Mark 5:1-20; Luke 8:26-39; Matt. 8:28-34 [Matthew notes that there were two men living among the tombs]). When Jesus came near and commanded the demon to leave the man, the man collapsed at the feet of Jesus and screamed, "What do you want with me, Jesus, Son of the Most High God? I beg you, don't torture me!" (Luke 8:28).

The demons told Jesus there were many of their kind inhabiting this man's heart, soul, mind, and strength. They begged Jesus to act with mercy on their behalf, asking him not to send them to the abyss in which they'd spend eternity.

The man had become like one of those once-gracious mansions that exist in neglected, rough corners of urban cores. Envision a massive old home that's been subdivided into a shady single-room-occupancy hotel and every room in the joint is occupied by a guest named either Hatfield or McCoy. Nonstop brawling is the result.

Jesus acted with compassion on this demon-occupied man's behalf by sending the demons into a nearby herd of swine. En masse, the crazed pigs stampeded down the hillside and drowned in the nearest abyss, the Sea of Galilee. Terrified, the men herding the pigs ran into the town to report what they'd witnessed.

The villagers headed to the tombs outside town and found the once-possessed man dressed and conversing with Jesus. Jesus demonstrated the nature of God's kingdom by evicting all of the flophouse tenants from the man's soul, knocking down the dividing walls the demons had erected in his heart, and welcoming the man to again be at home in his own body.

The villagers were terrified by the deliverance and begged Jesus to leave the vicinity. The man pleaded with Jesus to go with him, but Jesus told him to return home to tell his story. In a beautiful picture of the effect of his interior renovation, "The man went away and told all over town how much Jesus had done for him" (Luke 8:39).

A Full Life

When you hear Jesus' familiar words in John 10:10 ("The thief comes only to steal and kill and destroy; I have come that they may have life, and have it to the full"), what images come to your mind?

Some Bible teachers and preachers tell us this full, abundant life equals overflowing material blessing. Others tell us that it means personal fulfillment or a flourishing community characterized by a commitment to biblical justice.

Simply put, Jesus' words about himself reflect the values of the kingdom to which he was inviting each one of us. It is life brimming with God's goodness. It is flourishing life that reflects his glory. It is a reunited life where spooky, subdivided mansions become a gracious home once again.

This abundance has little to do with our circumstances, stuff, or surroundings. Jesus didn't put conditions on his words: "'I have come that they may have life, and have it to the full'—except when your husband has gambled away the proceeds from his business, your mom is in need of ongoing medical attention, your daughter got caught smoking weed, and you had an abortion."

It is possible to experience abundant life in the midst of the mess and muck of everyday life. It takes a united heart to be able to contain that abundance.

Most of us learn to limp along quite well with a divided heart. Insecurity, unforgiveness, idolatry, and anger will split our hearts into pieces.

As Deanna discovered, so will attempting to bury regret. The desire to "get on with her life" after the abortion kept her from dealing with painful "if onlys." Out of sight, out of mind, she'd hoped. So she compartmentalized her heart and buried her secret in a vault. No one else knew, but she could never quite forget. "If only" surfaced at the most inconvenient times—as she was drifting off to sleep, on the anniversary date of the abortion, once in a while when she helped out in the church nursery. Each time, she chased the "if only" back into the vault. The net effect was that she learned that getting on with her life was a high-maintenance proposition. She felt she didn't deserve peace after what she'd done in college, so maintaining a truce by keeping the past in the past would have to do. She recognized that this strategy wasn't ideal, but it was what her regrets told her she had coming to her.

The apostle Paul told his believing friends at Philippi that God was at work on their behalf, protecting their hearts and minds: "And the peace of God, which transcends all understanding, will guard your hearts and your minds in Christ Jesus" (Phil. 4:7). The peace to which he referred wasn't a truce, nor was it a blissed-out zone of calm.

The word "peace" (eirene) Paul used is an active word that can refer to agreement between nations, harmony between individuals, the state of eternal rest after death for believers, and salvation. The word eirene has its roots in the word "join." Paul tells us that the supernatural rejoining work of God in our lives acts as a sentry to protect from attack the most vulnerable parts of who we are: our hearts and minds.

Peace describes the relationship when two parties once estranged from each other are reunited, kintsugi-style—even if those parties are the divided places in our own hearts.

Reflection Questions

1. Have you ever made a conscious decision to keep something from your past "in a vault"? Were you able to do so?

2. How might the man set free from demons by Jesus have described the experience? Have you ever used words like this to describe the work of God in your own life? In what way?

3. Philippians 4:7 ("And the peace of God, which transcends all understanding, will guard your hearts and your minds in Christ Jesus") tells us that God's peace acts as a sentry in our lives. How so?

4. In what ways have you understood Jesus' promise of abundant life in the past? Has this promise matched your experience in the Christian life?

Prayer

Father, I have sometimes mislabeled my own human attempts to form a truce with my past as your peace. But if I keep it in the vault, I am acting as my own guard over that past, aren't I? And I am not such a good guard, because when I'm not expecting it, the past escapes and mocks me. It takes a lot of energy to keep that past in its place.

I think about that man living naked among the tombs outside of town. I cannot imagine the torment of heart and mind he must have experienced. He didn't just wake up one day like this. Reality slipped from his desperate grasp as the voices—there were so many voices!—shrieked a cacophony of lies at him.

And then you came and with a single word evicted all the squatters who'd infiltrated this man and knocked down all of those dividing walls housing them all. Every one of those false, fleabag rooms in his soul must have had a secret stashed inside; every one must have contained a rotting lie.

A truce could not set this man free. Only you, Prince of Peace, could do this.

Only you.

There are lots of things that divide my heart, Lord, including the "if onlys" I've buried there for safekeeping. I don't want to live this way anymore. Do what only you can do in me.

I again pray the words of David: "Teach me your way, Lord, that I may rely on your faithfulness; give me an undivided heart, that I may fear your name" (Ps. 86:11). I ask this because it reflects your character, perfect in love three-in-one—Father, Son, and Holy Spirit.

SEVEN

THE TRUTH, THE WHOLE TRUTH, AND NOTHING BUT THE TRUTH

THE CONFESSION CURE

*Few things accelerate the peace process
as much as humbly admitting our own
wrongdoing and asking forgiveness.*
—Lee Strobel

Even when the vault seems to be unlocked, we may find ourselves stucker-than-stuck in some area of our lives and not quite sure how we got there. If only we could figure out how to climb out of that quagmire.

My friend Heather and I figured it might be easier to climb out of that quagmire if we did it together. I adored her candor. Heather was as transparent as a sheet of glass, and her transparency made it easy for me to be honest with her too.

"I ate a half gallon of ice cream last night, then took a bunch of laxatives to clean it out of me. I hate myself this morning. I'm so stressed out with my new job, and Justin and I are having problems again. Would you pray with me? I need God's help."

We were both in our twenties, trying to figure out how to be grown-ups. Her honesty played well with my empathy and gave me the "gift of going second" in our relationship. Heather would share a struggle or failure, and I'd respond with one or two of my own.

We were like a two-person twelve-step self-help group. Except Sinners Anonymous members Heather and I were perpetually stuck at step one. We frequently admitted our powerlessness to one another, but we went no further. There were no steps two through twelve. No U-turns.

Her emotional phone calls invariably followed the same script. "You'll never believe what I did over the weekend," she wailed. "I did it again. Again! Ate most of the leftover pizza after Justin went to bed, then did a laxative chaser."

Money was very tight for my husband and me. I was constantly robbing Peter to pay Paul, then borrowing money from Paul to buy milk and diapers. I frequently confessed to Heather how I struggled to trust God with our finances. I had my own script I rehearsed with her most every time we talked.

It slowly dawned on me that all this confession wasn't really changing either of us. It was as though each one of us were taking emotional laxatives. Each of us was able to regularly expose and attempt to expel some of our issues in our conversations, but mostly we just named and rehearsed our sins. As a result, neither of us seemed to be able to go beyond the surface of encouraging one another toward meaningful repentance. Our struggles seemed to remain our struggles. I can't speak for Heather, but the longer I struggled and failed to experience any meaningful change, the more regrets I accumulated while I stayed mired in my sin.

Author Oscar Wilde diagnosed Heather and me with these words written over one hundred years ago: "There is a luxury in self-reproach. When we blame ourselves, we feel that no one else has a right to blame us."

I'd convinced myself that talking about my guilt with my friend was equivalent to repenting of my sin. However, not all confession is created equal. It can mean anything from recounting the details of a crime we've committed to revealing a gossipy tidbit to a friend.

The truth is, Heather and I spent a whole lot of our time gossiping about ourselves to each other.

'Fessing Up

Writer Martha Beck observed, "We all have a deep psychological need to be accepted as we really are, but that can never happen as long as there are parts of us that no one sees or knows. We conceal aspects of ourselves that we think invite rejection, but ironically, the very act of secrecy makes us inaccessible to love. We think we're hiding our secrets, but really, our secrets are hiding us."[1]

Confession is good for us. It puts us in touch with our own weaknesses and flaws. Every one of us has a tendency to minimize our own failings and magnify the failings of others. Confession levels the playing field. It also cleanses our conscience—our mind's memory and response to what is right and wrong. When we lug our unconfessed wrongdoing around with us, it takes up unwelcome space in our brain.

Confession is a teacher. The discomfort of confession can help us retrain our bad habits. One of my sons once stole a small toy from a local bookstore. The conviction of the Holy Spirit pressed on his guilty conscience until he told me what he'd done. I took him to the store and briefly explained the situation to the store manager. She invited us into her office, where my teary-eyed son confessed to the theft and returned the toy. He'd brought some of his allowance money to repay the store as well. The discomfort brought his budding shoplifting career to an end.

Finally, confession is an antidote for fear. I discovered an especially sad example of what happens when fear prevents us from stepping into the light to tell the truth in the story of a Serbian man named Janez Rus. Rus had collaborated with the German army during World War II against the Communist forces that would become the ruling government in Rus's country. He was so afraid of what might happen to him if he came forward after the war that he went into hiding in his sister's rural farmhouse attic.

Weeks turned into months. Months stretched into years—thirty-two years, to be precise. "Throughout these years, I did nothing and never left the house," he later told a reporter. "Through the windows, I looked down to the villages in the valley. People seldom passed by our house which is isolated in the hills. When I heard happy people singing I cried."

Sixty-four-year-old Rus was discovered in 1978 and learned at that time no charges had ever been filed against him. One official noted, "He sentenced himself to a punishment which no court could pass on him."[2]

The courage to step forward and confess could have granted him an early release from the prison of his own fears.

Confession God's Way

Richard Foster noted in his classic work *Celebration of Discipline* that not all confession brings us into right relationship with God. "Without the cross . . . confession would be only psychologically therapeutic. But it is so much more. It involves an objective change in our relationship with God and a subjective change in us. It is a means of healing and transforming the inner spirit."[3]

When we recognize that our sin offends our holy God, and we acknowledge in gratitude that he sent his Son to the cross to take the punishment each one of us deserves, confession moves beyond a psychological release to an act of humble obedience.

"Confession's primary purpose is not to set us straight, give other people satisfaction in our shame, or make it easier for God to forgive us," writer Amy Simpson said. "It's to show us our sin. To show us who we are, in comparison not to others, but to our perfect, holy God. And to help us understand the undeserved grace he extends every single time. We who most need to see our own sin are the ones most tempted to think we're not that bad."[4]

Biblical truths about confession are rooted in an affirmation of belief in the risen Christ: "If you declare with your mouth, 'Jesus is Lord,' and believe in your heart that God raised him from the dead, you will be saved" (Rom. 10:9). This affirmation of God's work in our lives may take the form of sharing the story of my faith journey with another person, or it may mean a more formal verbal congregational affirmation of a creed during a Sunday morning worship service. But at its heart, spiritual confession is always an outflow of what my heart knows is true about God and about myself.

Spiritual confession means that we are acting on this conviction: "If we claim to be without sin, we deceive ourselves and the truth is not in us. If we confess our sins, he is faithful and just and will forgive us our sins and purify us from all unrighteousness. If we claim we have not sinned, we make him out to be a liar and his word is not in us" (1 John 1:8-10).

Confession is a key component of repentance, of changing direction in order to turn from our sin and return to our God. Jesus' cousin John had one message meant to prepare people for the coming of their long-awaited Savior: "Repent, for the kingdom of heaven has come near" (Matt. 3:2).

The idea of repentance is deeply embedded in Jewish culture. From the beginning, the story of the chosen people was often a cycle of the people falling away from God and then returning to him. This was rarely their first idea; God used the consequences of illness and warfare with surrounding nations to help them adopt the idea for themselves. The temple offering system provided the people a clear path in which they could acknowledge their sinfulness before God and return to relationship with him.

Each year, the Jewish New Year (Rosh Hashanah) still launches a ten-day period of focused introspection and repentance leading up to the most sacred day in the Jewish calendar, Yom Kippur, or the Day of Atonement. This was the one day each year in which the high priest would enter the holy of holies and sacrifice a spotless, perfect offering to God, confessing the sins of his people and pleading for God's forgiveness for all. At the cross, Jesus acted as our priest, interceding for us before his Father while at the same time becoming the spotless, perfect sacrifice. We are forgiven.

Because of what he has done for us, we can come back to God. We can be restored. God himself gives us the gift of repentance (2 Tim. 2:25). It demands change from us. Sometimes we welcome that change. Other times, we may be afraid it will be too much, too hard, too humbling. At other times, our regrets handcuff us to the past so we can't fully extend our hands to receive what God longs to give us.

Confession is how we respond to his gift of repentance. King David models wholehearted confession in the prayer he wrote after the prophet Nathan confronted him about what he'd done to Bathsheba and her husband, Uriah:

> Have mercy on me, O God, according to your unfailing love; according to your great compassion blot out my transgressions. Wash away all my iniquity and cleanse me from my sin. For I know my transgressions, and my sin is always before me. Against you, you only, have I sinned and done what is evil in

your sight; so you are right in your verdict and justified when you judge. (Ps. 51:1-4)

Bible teacher Vance Havner said,

We are sometimes repentant because of the harm we have done ourselves and others in our transgressions but there is little repentance toward God . . . We may regret what our sins do to our testimony and the evil effect on others but we are little concerned because the fellowship with God is broken. This makes for shallow and inadequate confession because we have not touched the heart of the trouble.[5]

Confession moves beyond the therapeutic when it begins with the way we've damaged our relationship with a holy God. If it doesn't, we may reap some of its emotional benefits, but our sin remains unexposed—still festering, still wreaking havoc in our lives. It was a lesson my friend Heather and I needed to learn in our odd two-woman version of a self-help group that actually wasn't helping either of us much at all.

Halfway There

The story of Jonah, the reluctant prophet, offers a helpful picture of the way a "nearly there" confession can carry us almost—almost, but not all the way—to the place we most need to go. God tapped Jonah in the eighth century before Christ's birth to leave his home in northern Israel and travel east five hundred or so miles to the Assyrian city of Nineveh (modern-day Iraq). God had a message for the idol-worshipping Ninevites, and he chose Jonah to deliver it.

Jonah balked at God's command to him. Jonah loathed the idol-worshipping, warring Assyrians and couldn't imagine why God would bother to say anything to the enemies of his people.

So Jonah voted with his feet even though the polls on the subject were not open. He responded to God's command to him by doing the opposite. Jonah headed west and boarded a ship to carry him to Tarshish, which was located in what is now Spain. It was about as far as he could go in the opposite direction from Assyria.

In the midst of a violent storm at sea, Jonah confessed to the ship's crew that he was running from God (Jonah 1:9-10). Jonah told the crew he could solve their problem (and perhaps add the bonus of an instant cure for the remorse he must have been feeling as the ship tossed violently in the maelstrom) by throwing him overboard. Jonah was willing to sacrifice his life to save theirs, which says something of the kind of man God knew he could be when Jonah wasn't running as fast as he could away from him.

The crew threw him overboard, and the sea stilled as Jonah disappeared into the mouth of a giant sea beast.

God was not done with Jonah, as Jonah's improbable survival inside the beast testifies. It is at this point that Jonah confesses his sin and submits to do what God had asked him to do back in Israel: "What I have vowed I will make good. I will say, 'Salvation comes from the Lord'" (Jonah 2:9). In response, the fish vomited him onto a beach and (after a bath) Jonah made his way to Nineveh.

He walked the breadth of the sprawling Assyrian city, calling on them to repent. They did. These enemies of God's people grieved their sin. Their king stripped off his royal robes, donned sackcloth, and prostrated himself in the dust before God. From this lower-than-low position, he issued an order that required everyone in the city to fast, mourn, and seek Jonah's God in repentance.

Imagine one man's message changing the spiritual culture of an entire city! It went better than Jonah ever could have dreamed, which, as it turns out, was exactly what he was afraid of way back when this whole adventure began. Jonah was furious that the Ninevites had joined the One True God team.

That was supposed to be Jonah's team.

The thought of all of these new teammates peeled away the iron barricade protecting the corner of Jonah's heart that had abstained from repenting while Jonah cried out to God from the belly of the sea beast. That 95 percent repentance carried Jonah all the way to Nineveh. The other 5 percent—the barricade of fear, anger, and prejudice—led him to repeat the cycle and do what he knew how to do best.

He ran.

He headed into the blazing, barren desert outside Nineveh and asked to die (Jonah 4:3). In response, God sent a supernaturally fast-growing plant to shade Jonah. Some of Jonah's self-pity began to dissipate in the relative cool of the shade. In this moment, God destroyed the plant. Jonah was again exposed, and he confessed the nature of his heart's barricade. He told God he wished he were dead rather than living in a world where God's mercy triumphed over Jonah's sense of justice. If ever there was a picture of regret's fruit in full flower, it is Jonah sitting beside this withered vine. Nothing had gone the way Jonah really, truly wished it would have.

God knew all along exactly what kind of issues Jonah was harboring behind that barricade in his heart. And yet, he chose to use Jonah despite the way Jonah had fled from God, despite his imperfect repentance, his prejudices, and his lack of compassion.

The book of Jonah ends abruptly. God has the final word, in the form of a question. And this question vaults over that crumbling barricade of Jonah's into the 5 percent of Jonah's heart he'd exempted from full repentance. God's question demonstrates his love for every bit of his creation: "Should I not have concern for the great city of Nineveh, in which there are more than a hundred and twenty thousand people who cannot tell their right hand from their left—and also many animals?" (Jonah 4:11).

We are left to imagine Jonah's response. That these words are recorded in Scripture when Jonah was the only witness to them suggests to me that he repented 100 percent. I believe he turned away from his sin and wholly and completely turned to God.

Just like the people of Nineveh had.

Tell It Straight

The Holy Spirit will convict you of your sin (John 16:8-9). This conviction comes from the Father's love for you (1 John 4:9-11). Your forgiveness has been secured for you in the work of Christ on the cross (Rom. 5:8). Confession is the way we agree with God about who he is, who we are, and how we understand that what we've done has rent our relationship with him.

Some find the way to best express their contrition to God is by simply naming it in their own words in prayer. Others find just the right words they need in the liturgical prayers of confession used in some church traditions. Meditating on Scripture and journaling can be a springboard to confession as well.

There is great power in going to another person in order to haul a sin festering in the darkness to the light of day. While I recognize there is a temptation in a few relationships to become an echo chamber, parroting our sins back and forth to one another as Heather and I did, the reality is that a desire to get it straight with the Lord can't be disentangled from the call to humble ourselves before him (James 4:4-10). God uses his community of believers in order to restore us to himself: "Confess your sins to each other and pray for each other so that you may be healed. The prayer of a righteous person is powerful and effective" (James 5:16).

It's also important to remember that not all confessions bring full restoration to a broken relationship. Not every confession will heal damaged trust.

Several years after ending up on opposite sides of a painful church division, a couple of former friends of ours appeared on our doorstep. My husband and I had once been very close with both. We'd done what we could to maintain the relationship, but they'd decided to end the friendship without a word of explanation.

When they came to our home, they did so in order to confess that they'd been cowards. Their "if onlys" had been haunting them. "We were afraid of what the others involved in the church conflict would have thought of us if we continued to be friends with you, since you were perceived by them to be on the 'wrong side.' We were scared to think for ourselves. It was immature of us, and we were wrong. Would you forgive us?"

We were happy to forgive them, although those friendships would never be the same. Too much time had passed, and our lives had moved in different directions from theirs. But our fellowship was restored, for which my husband and I are exceedingly grateful.

Jesus gave us a pattern for prayer that is grounded in community. He never expected us to pray the words of the Lord's Prayer, found in Matthew 6:9-13, in the first person singular. Imagine it: "My Father who art in heaven . . . give me today my daily bread, forgive me my debts as I forgive my debtors, and lead me from temptation and deliver me from the evil one . . ."

I have certainly asked God for each of those things for myself plenty of times over the years. But the "us" of this prayer is echoed again and again throughout the New Testament. We are a body (1 Cor. 12:12-14), and we flourish as individuals as we serve and worship together. And when we aren't flourishing—when one of us is ill or bound in sin—we're encouraged to confess our sins to one another in order to pray for each other (James 5:13-16).

Turning and returning to God often includes others in the process. In some cases, you may need to tell the truth to another person about something you've done to wrong him or her in order to seek the person's forgiveness. His purpose for us is always reconciliation with himself—and if at all possible, with others (Rom. 12:18). In Christ, we are forgiven.

While admitting our guilt to our merciful God is always the right thing to do, it is worth remembering that not everything can be confessed to others, nor should it be. If the individual to whom you wish to confess has died, for example, you won't be able to talk to the person. If you've daydreamed about being in a relationship with a man other than your husband, you may not need to confess this—but you may well need to ask God to show you why this is going on inside of you, then prepare yourself for what the Holy Spirit may expose in you so that you can live your repentance.

I acknowledge that confessing your sin to another person or to a group of people can be a risky proposition. Your confession might become fodder for gossip. Someone might place you in a box and label you with the name of your sin. You might share your story with someone who doesn't have any desire to do anything but tell you you're a victim and wallow in self-pity with you.

I've known people whose biggest regrets are tied to confessing something to a mean or immature person. What can be a tricky part of this deal is that you may not find out you've entrusted your pearls to swine until after the swine have trampled them to smithereens.

I believe there are greater risks in not living this way. Verbalizing our sin to another person has the power to help us get to the bottom of what might be keeping us from receiving God's mercy. My long-time prayer partner, Meg, is not afraid to ask me hard questions in order to probe beyond my own attempts at low-octane confessions. God has used her on many occasions over the years to reveal the 5 percent my pride has told me I must keep tucked away in my heart for safekeeping. It is that wee bit of unconfessed sin that acts as fertilizer for my regrets, allowing them to grow like thistles.

Cutting off the flow of fertilizer can staunch the growth of those thistles, but eradicating them requires us to don a thick pair of gloves so we can pull those prickly plants from the soil by the roots.

Reflection Questions

1. How has God used the experience of confession to teach or train you?

2. When have you seen evidence—either in your own life or in the life of another person—that a confession wasn't entirely sincere?

3. How would you describe the relationship between confession and repentance?

4. Have you ever been hurt after you've confessed something to someone else and then had your words used to either become a source of gossip about you or to unjustly label you? How? What did the experience teach you? How do you reconcile it with what Scripture tells you about the importance of confession?

Prayer

You are holy, O God. There is no one like you. You have created all things, and you yourself came to redeem all things through the blood your Son shed on the cross.

You came to save me.

In you, Jesus, is life, and your life is the light for each one of us (John 1:4). Wherever you are, darkness cannot exist. You know the truth about me, right down to the secrets hiding within each atom of my body. "If I say, 'Surely the darkness will hide me and the light become night around me,' even the darkness will not be dark to you; the night will shine like the day, for darkness is as light to you" (Ps. 139:11-12). There is no place to hide from you.

And when I confess my sin to you, I am humbly admitting that this is true—that you are true. There is nothing hidden from your sight, nothing you don't know, nothing that will surprise or shock or repulse you about me. Please open my ears when I open my mouth to confess, so that I can hear you pronounce me forgiven.

Forgiven.

That word, fulfilled in your Son. For me.

Forgiven.

Nothing separating me from your love and mercy.

Forgiven.

Thank you.

EIGHT

TRUCE LIKE A RIVER?

THE PEACE THAT CROSSES OUR DIVIDING WALLS

Heart knows no sorrow like the sorrow of regretting.
—Martha Lavinia Hoffman

Have you ever wandered through a crowd searching for someone—say, at a busy mall or a sporting event—and when you turn around, there the person is, standing right behind you?

The experience is a sweet jolt, isn't it?

Confession is the way in which we acknowledge we're in search of forgiveness. As we agree with God about our sin, it's like being in a crowd, then turning around, and oh! There he is!

And we discover that Jesus was right behind us, waiting for us to turn around and see him standing there.

The truth is, he came looking for us even before we started searching for him (Luke 19:10). His search-and-rescue mission has more to do with every single one of our "if onlys" than most of us could have ever dreamed.

Throwing Stones . . . or Not

She stood before the ad hoc tribunal in the blazing sunlight. No question that she was guilty. Guilty as sin.

The man with whom she shared a bed—not her husband—seems to have skittered into the shadows. She was alone. Miss Caught-in-the-Act gave the religious authorities a perfect, efficient opportunity to take care of two problems at once. They could dispatch God's justice to this law-breaking adulteress and entrap Jesus at the same time. Odds were that whatever Jesus said about her sin would more than likely give them enough ammunition to indict him too.

John 7:53—8:11 records this account. This story doesn't appear in the earliest manuscripts of the Bible and is usually presented with an asterisk or in brackets of some kind in most modern translations because of its unclear provenance. However, few dispute that the story reflects Christ's character and his ministry to sinners of all kinds.

As we see in other places in Scripture (such as Matt. 22:15-36), the religious authorities were committed to entrapping Jesus with his own words. In their estimation, he'd been wayyyy too cozy with sinners and wayyyy too sloppy in his interpretation of the Law. The Torah prescribed stoning to death as the appropriate punishment for her sin. No ifs, ands, or buts.

There was no opportunity in this Judean "courtroom" for the woman to tell her side of the story; there was no defense attorney to ask her what led her to share her bed with a man not her husband. Did she have a family that might want to stand with her? Or had she always been on her own, practicing the world's oldest profession so she could simply survive? Did she wonder why her lover wasn't receiving the same treatment she was?

Of one thing I'm certain: she'd already put herself on trial, long before she stood shivering with fear in the blazing midday sun, surrounded by a jury of the most ferociously righteous religious experts in the city. It's my sense that she probably had no reason to expect Jesus would utter a word of dissent in this matter.

She may not have known Jesus had already scandalized various members of this hastily assembled kangaroo court by healing on the Sabbath (Mark 3:1-6), fellowshipping with "untouchable" sinners (Luke 5:27-29), and celebrating the wholehearted devotion of another woman with a questionable history (Luke 7:36-50).

After one of the religious authorities stated the charges against the woman, the parallel "unofficial" trial of Jesus got underway. All eyes moved from the forlorn figure of the woman to Jesus, who was squatting on his haunches, drawing in the dust with his finger. What would he say?

"Let any one of you who is without sin be the first to throw a stone at her" (John 8:7). The words were a bolt of lightning out of a cloudless blue sky. He bent to the dust. And he waited.

One by one, the accusers walked away until Jesus was left standing alone with this woman clothed in shame and regret. He asked her where all her accusers had gone. When she replied that no one was left there to condemn her, I wonder: Did she include herself on that list?

Jesus made it impossible for her to walk away from the episode and later imprison herself in regret. Instead, Jesus' words to her are words of peace and freedom: "'Then neither do I condemn you,' Jesus declared. 'Go now and leave your life of sin'" (v. 11).

Even more shocking, Jesus said basically the same words to Saul, a man who didn't think he was a sinner until he was blindsided on the road to Damascus a half-handful of years after this woman caught in adultery had been given a new lease on life (Acts 9:1-19). Saul violated rules he was bound to enforce but was unable to keep. After his surrender to the One who sought him on that road, Saul, now called Paul by God, spoke eloquently about his own spiritual imprisonment:

So I find this law at work: Although I want to do good, evil is right there with me. For in my inner being I delight in God's law; but I see another law at work in me, waging war against the law of my mind and making me a prisoner of the law of sin at work within me. What a wretched man I am! Who will rescue me from this body that is subject to death? Thanks be to God, who delivers me through Jesus Christ our Lord! . . .

Therefore, there is now no condemnation for those who are in Christ Jesus, because through Christ Jesus the law of the Spirit who gives life has set you free from the law of sin and death. For what the law was powerless to do because it was weakened by the flesh, God did by sending his own Son in the likeness of sinful flesh to be a sin offering. (Rom. 7:21—8:3)

Underneath Paul's carefully scripted religious exterior beat a heart as divided and sinful as the woman's. Both Paul and the woman caught red-handed in the sin of adultery each heard *the exact same message* from Jesus.

Though they couldn't have been more different, Jesus declared each of them innocent, even though each of them was in fact guilty in God's sight.

"Neither do I condemn you," Jesus told the woman.

"No condemnation for those who are in Christ Jesus!" Paul proclaimed the forgiveness he'd been given to anyone who would listen—and lots of people who wouldn't.

Amazing Grace

We do love "once was lost, now am found" stories of sin and God's mercy, don't we? Yet we aren't always so sure what to do with the regrets that accumulate after we've been found, are we?

What would we say to the woman caught in adultery if we learned that six months after her life-saving encounter with Jesus she'd gotten involved with another lover or two? How would we respond to Paul if we heard that he'd shrugged off his encounter with Jesus as merely a heat-induced hallucination and that he'd gone back to his former habits, persecuting believers?

What do we say to ourselves when we've done things we've regretted after we've heard Jesus pronounce us forgiven?

Before his death by hanging in a Nazi death camp in 1945, Pastor Dietrich Bonhoeffer wrote about the ways in which we may be tempted to devalue the priceless words "Neither do I condemn you" in our lives. He called this "cheap grace":

Cheap grace . . . amounts to the justification of sin without the justification of the repentant sinner who departs from sin and from whom sin departs. Cheap grace is not the kind of forgiveness of sin which frees us from the toils of sin. Cheap grace is the grace we bestow on ourselves.

Cheap grace is grace without discipleship, grace without the cross, grace without Jesus Christ, living and incarnate.[1]

Bonhoeffer's firm and truthful words remind us that cheap grace simply moves us from one jail cell to another. He reminds us that cheap grace is nothing more than a flimsy, breakable plastic key incapable of unlocking the shut-tight lock on our cell.

Normally, we think of cheap grace as the kind of ersatz mercy that refuses to call sin what it is in the name of "love." But we can also put a price tag on grace when we put our own boundaries and limits on it. We cheapen God's costly grace when we insist that our regrets disqualify us from receiving his mercy. We devalue it when we declare our sin greater than Christ's forgiveness. I did this in the months and years following my decision to shush God's voice the day my youngest son was born. I lived with the wrong belief that God was tolerating me as long as I brought to the party as my guest the condemnation I so richly deserved. In doing so, I put a mark-down price tag on his priceless grace.

Christ never said he was gritting his teeth and putting up with me. He knew exactly who I was, am, and will be when he showed me he loved me without condition.

The Message paraphrase of Romans 5:6-8 captures the past, present, and future of this perfect and costly love:

Christ arrives right on time to make this happen. He didn't, and doesn't, wait for us to get ready. He presented himself for this sacrificial death when we were far too weak and rebellious to do anything to get ourselves ready. And even if we hadn't been so weak, we wouldn't have known what to do anyway. We can understand someone dying for a person worth dying for, and we can understand how someone good and noble could inspire us to selfless sacrifice. But God put his love on the line for us by offering his Son in sacrificial death while we were of no use whatever to him.

Sometimes we end up in spiritual bankruptcy even when it appears to the rest of the world that we're doing well. My friend Hope had a life that appeared to me to be "an untarnished success story." She told me why this was the case: "I was so afraid of getting it wrong." The "it" to which she referred included career, friendships, spouse, church, and parenting decisions. "On the outside, it looked like I was doing all the right things," she said. "But I was doing those things for all the wrong reasons."

And then the veneer of all of that right living was pierced when she brought her mother, diagnosed with Alzheimer's, into her home to live. "See? It was the right thing to do, but I did it because I was afraid that if I didn't, people would say I was a bad Christian." The stress of caring for her mom on a day-in, day-out basis caused Hope to reconsider the way she'd lived her life to that point. "I realized I was so afraid of doing something I'd regret later. I thought I was fearing God by making the choices I made, but I slowly realized that mostly, I was fearing fear."

There was a period when she dreamed of what her life might have been if she weren't so afraid of getting it wrong. "There is nothing like helping your mom toilet herself to set your imagination free," she remarked wryly. The years spent caring for her mom gave her plenty of opportunity to reflect on what her life might have been if fear had not been a factor in the choices she made when she was young. "Those dreams of what might have been are always better than the life we're living, aren't they?"

Hope discovered it wasn't easy to dismiss her woulda, coulda, shoulda thoughts in the emotional pressure cooker of being a caregiver. Her "if onlys" left her in turmoil. Every time she'd made the right choice for the wrong reason, the choice added to the divisions in her heart. She never realized those divisions existed at the level they did until regrets alerted her to their presence.

The Prince of Peace

At the final Passover meal he shared with his disciples, Jesus promised that after he left them, he'd send the Holy Spirit to us as a teacher, counselor, and advocate (John 14:26). Coupled with that promise, Jesus gave his disciples the blessing of his peace. "Peace I leave with you; my peace I give you. I do not give to you as the world gives. Do not let your hearts be troubled and do not be afraid" (v. 27).

For years when I read those words, I imagined that he was giving them the gift of a very tranquil mood. I used to wonder if I'd disconnected from God if I was anything other than Hawaiian sunset calm. (For the record, I am not by nature a Hawaiian sunset calm sort of person.) I imagined that Jesus had what I assumed was the ideal temperament—a placid, sanguine personality. What he meant with his words about giving his followers his peace, then, was that he would magically overwrite my own slightly more volatile wiring with his serenity.

Though peace certainly has an emotional component to it, those tranquil emotions are a side dish, not the main course. Jesus was speaking about something more comprehensive, and the kind of peace he promises speaks directly to the cause and the effect of the regrets in our lives.

As he was preparing to leave his friends, he was giving them his *shalom*. In the process, he was redefining it for them. *Shalom* is a word used for both "hello" and "good-bye" in Jewish culture. It means far more than just "Whassup?" or "See ya later." It is a word that means peace. It was used (and still is, in some circles of the Jewish community) as a shorthand prayer of blessing for another person. The root of the noun *shalom* is the verb *shaleim*, which means "to restore." It is the ancient Hebrew word for the New Testament Greek word *eirene*, with its roots in "to join"—which we first visited in chapter 6.

Theologian Cornelius Plantinga writes,

The word *shalom* paints a picture of safety, prosperity, completion, and wholeness. In the Bible, shalom means *universal flourishing, wholeness, and delight*—a rich state of affairs in which natural needs are satisfied and natural gifts fruitfully employed, a state of affairs that inspires joyful wonder as its Creator and Savior opens doors and welcomes the creatures in whom he delights. Shalom, in other words, is the way things ought to be.[2]

When Jesus told his disciples he was leaving them with his peace, he was telling them he was giving them the priceless gift of a restored relationship with God. Past, present, and future, the Prince of Peace came to make us whole (Isa. 9:6).

Regrets fragment our hearts. Perhaps because I'd long believed that God's peace primarily described a placid emotional state, I figured the best way to deal with my regrets that most definitely didn't leave me feeling at all peaceful was to avoid dealing with them. Keeping them buried behind walls in my heart seemed a sure way to stay at peace. I'd read passages such as Psalm 103:11-12 ("For as high as the heavens are above the earth, so great is his love for those who fear him; as far as the east is from the west, so far has he removed our transgressions from us") and I would tell myself that if God said he forgave me, then I just needed to act like that calm Hawaiian sunset scene—or else! I missed the fact that God was the one doing the work of reconciliation.

As I began to ponder the true meaning of shalom, I realized that wholeness can only come as I submit to God and he reconnects all of the fragmented pieces of my past. This wholeness means I will flourish in the present and be free to follow Christ into the future without fear or false limitations.

Job described his reclamation mission with these words: "He reveals the deep things of darkness and brings utter darkness into the light" (Job 12:22). David knew a thing or two about God's pursuit of him, regrets and all. He expressed it beautifully when he wrote, "If I say, 'Surely the darkness will hide me and the light become night around me,' even the darkness will not be dark to you; the night will shine like the day, for darkness is as light to you" (Ps. 139:11-12).

The work of shalom demanded I stop avoiding my "if onlys." The Prince of Peace wanted to stand with me in order to face my regrets. His Spirit would teach me how the Father would reclaim what I'd buried there.

He knew far better than I did what was on the far side of those dividing walls I'd erected with such precision in my heart.

Reflection Questions

1. What is most shocking to you about Jesus' pronouncement of "no condemnation" to both the woman caught in adultery and to Saul? Why?

2. How might putting our own artificial limits on God's grace cheapen it? When have you seen this in action?

3. How have you viewed Christians once known for their strong convictions or great faith who had harbored a secret, sinful side that was later revealed?

4. Has your expectation that God's peace is limited to the realm of emotions gotten in the way of the entire scope of what *shalom/eirene* really means?

Prayer

I recognize that my sin puts me at war with you, O God. It is a war I can never win.

You sent your Son to end the war. The Prince of Peace stepped into this battle and cried out, "It is finished" (John 19:30). You came to save each one of us who trusts in you to do so. You tell us we are no longer condemned to perish in this war.

Please give me ears to hear. Please help me to live in light of what I hear. I don't want to cheapen your grace by sinning. Nor do I wish to cheapen your mercy by believing that my sin is greater than your sacrifice.

You bless those who were once your enemies with your shalom. In the past, I have understood this shalom you give as some sort of spiritual mood stabilizer. I have made it smaller than it is, and I have contented myself to live in that smallness.

No more, Lord. Here I am. Unite my "if only"-divided heart so I can live a life that proclaims your peace. In the name of my Redeemer, your Son.

Amen.

NINE

WHEN THE PAST BECOMES THE PRESENT

WHY OUR HISTORY STILL TELLS TALES

There is no person so severely punished, as those who
subject themselves to the whip of their own remorse.

—Lucius Annaeus Seneca

· ·

We don't need to engage in endless introspection in order to search for the root of every regret. Let's face it: the genesis of most of our "if onlys" is fairly obvious. Other regrets may require a bit of reflection so that we trace them back to their beginnings, but they don't require a full archaeological excavation.

But there are times in our lives when some digging may be exactly what is needed. Otherwise, we are simply pulling the weed's flower and leaving the root to multiply and spread. At points of major life change, including death, divorce, relocation, catastrophic illness or injury, uprooting of our regularly scheduled lives happens whether or not we wish for it to occur. The disruption exposes the pain of dormant "if onlys" in ways we haven't been expecting.

Those ancient regrets may chain us to the past in ways we don't fully recognize until they're brought to light by the One who promises to set every captive free.

Jesus told us he has come to throw open every prison door. At the start of his public ministry, he read the prophet Isaiah's words to those assembled in his hometown synagogue:

The Spirit of the Lord is on me, because he has anointed me to proclaim good news to the poor. He has sent me to proclaim freedom for the prisoners and recovery of sight for the blind, to set the oppressed free, to proclaim the year of the Lord's favor. (Luke 4:18-19)

With every eye in the room on him, this carpenter's son told his hearers that this ancient promise was fulfilled that very day. This means Jesus can set us free from the regrets that have imprisoned us, perhaps in ways in which we're not even fully aware. The journey toward freedom may not look anything like what we imagine it to be when we read those dynamic words of Jesus in our Bibles.

Introspection will not set us free. But the path out of the prison of our past regrets might be created by allowing Christ to do his always-precise excavation of our lives.

I'd lived longer than I realized in a very comfy prison cell of regret until God used a death, an empty nest, and a rapid-fire series of family crises to redeem my past and renew my present. In the process, I discovered that the road to freedom wound in twisty directions I never could have anticipated.

There is nothing—not a single thing you currently claim as a regret—in your history that is beyond God's redemption.

This story is how I know this to be true.

Can You Keep a Secret?

A few weeks before my parents' wedding in 1957, my mom, then eighteen years old, got a phone call from George, a man she'd met a couple of times in passing during visits to New York City to see extended family. George told her that he really wanted to attend her upcoming wedding but hadn't been invited. She knew him as a distant cousin, so his request seemed to come from out of nowhere. And then he explained why he'd been compelled to ask with a single sentence that upended and scattered everything she'd ever believed true about her life.

"I am your father."

My mom didn't know she was adopted until she got that phone call. She never, ever talked about what happened in the hours and days after that traumatic phone call. What did the people who raised her, the only parents she'd ever known, say to her? What did she think? How did she feel?

My mom's birthmother, Molly, died shortly after giving birth to her. George had no idea how he would be able to care for a newborn in addition to his nine-year-old son. Several aunts and uncles who lived nearby stepped in to ensure that the boy would be cared for while George was at work. But a newborn baby needed so much more than any one of them could give her.

News of Molly's death spread through the grapevine of the extended family. At the distant end of that grapevine, Barbara, one of Molly's cousins who lived in Chicago, heard about the motherless child and believed this baby might just be the answer to her prayers. She and her husband, Louis, had never been able to have children, and she wanted a family more than anything. Louis was indifferent to the idea. He enjoyed his position as king of the household and wasn't particularly enthusiastic about the prospect of sharing his throne with a kid.

But Barbara eventually got him to agree to reach out to George. The pair let George know that they'd raise the baby as their own if, and only if, everyone in the family was sworn to secrecy. There was a very real stigma attached to adoption in those days, which may have fueled their request, but I suspect that Barbara wanted to ensure that their little girl would never for one moment question who her "real" parents were.

Desperate to find a safe place for the tiny baby, George and the rest of the family agreed to the plan. This was a no-win situation; any choice the grieving widower and father made was almost certain to leave him with regret. I've wondered what it was like the day he and his young son said good-bye to the last gift Molly gave to them and what those first weeks were like for Barbara and Louis as the little girl they named Gail joined them and they became a family of three.

George and the rest of the family kept close tabs on Gail's life in Chicago from afar. It is possible they may have occasionally been in the same room with her at an extended family gathering or two when Barbara and Louis visited family in New York City. How could those gatherings have not been incredibly awkward when everyone who knew the story was simultaneously tiptoeing around the secret while trying somehow to connect with this little girl who was a piece of their hearts?

The fact that Gail appeared well cared for was enough to communicate to them that she was doing well.

Except she wasn't OK. Louis was an alcoholic and Barbara the classic codependent. As a result, home was an unpredictable, unsafe place for Gail. Louis had become a father against his will, and he reminded Gail of it in a million unspoken ways. Barbara overcompensated for him, driving her daughter toward a perfectionist mind-set that had at its roots the idea that if only she could get it right somehow, maybe someone would love her.

She couldn't get it right. Every day was a reminder that she wasn't good enough, pretty enough—her flaws and imperfections were the unpardonable sin in her home. And if they weren't forgivable by the people who were supposed to love her most in the world, Gail learned at a young age how to protect herself behind an impenetrable barrier of fear, anger, and unforgiveness.

A product of her era, she headed to college just long enough to have a whirlwind romance and get engaged. It was, perhaps, her hope that she might be worth loving because this person found her lovable.

In the swirl of those wedding plans, the long fuse of regret, lit the day George agreed to relinquish his parental rights to Barbara and Louis, finally exploded in the form of a phone call. He just wanted to see Molly's baby girl walk down the aisle.

Passing on the Spiritual DNA

In addition to the sense of rejection she experienced in the home in which she was raised, the history-revising revelation of the truth about her origins and the disorientation she was experiencing over the family she'd lost convinced my mom that the only way she could survive her life was by barricading herself behind a wall of anger and bitterness. I've wondered if hiding behind that wall was the wish that she'd never been born.

My mom bragged throughout my childhood about how unforgiving she was, as if this were the highest virtue to which a person could aspire. Her deep wounds turned her into a very hurtful person. She told my sister and me how unattractive we were. She worried endlessly about what people would think of us. She berated us in front of others, hoping, perhaps, that they would recognize that any flaws we had were our own fault and didn't reflect poorly on her. She repeated what was most familiar to her from her own upbringing, passing it on just as she'd passed on Molly's blue eyes and George's curly hair to me.

I spent my childhood doing what I could to hide from my mom's acid words. There was nothing more that I craved than forgiveness; it was how I experienced love. While I often found myself frustrated that my dad didn't do more to protect my sister and me from my mom's hurtful words, his affection for us was an antidote to some of the emotional toxins swirling around our home. God used that longing for love and deep desire to know what was true to draw me to himself when I was a high school student.

Though they were not religiously observant, my Jewish parents were deeply offended by my newfound faith in Jesus the Messiah. While they didn't disown me, they distanced themselves emotionally from their Jesus Freak daughter. I'd always felt distant from them, so the additional separation didn't punish me as much as they imagined it might have.

I Should Have Told Someone

As I entered adulthood, I realized that in order to grow up in Christ, I needed to forgive—and keep on forgiving—my parents. I looked for a loophole in Jesus' words: "And when you stand praying, if you hold anything against anyone, forgive them, so that your Father in heaven may forgive you your sins" (Mark 11:25). There was no loophole. There was just the truth that forgiveness wasn't a once and done deal but was an ongoing process that might mean I would have to come back to the same choice whether or not to forgive "seventy times seven" times (Matt. 18:21-22; see NIV margin).

With God's help, I forgave and forgave again. At about point number 387 or so, it started getting easier. Every time I did, I grew in compassion for them, particularly my mom. While we were never close, I experienced genuine affection for them both.

My dad died on his sixty-fourth birthday, and my mom responded the only way she knew now—with additional anger. She was furious that my father had abandoned her and determined that no one would ever do that to her again. A few of her acquaintances told me over the years that they were a little scared of her. She never let them get too close. I understood exactly what they were talking about.

Eleven fairly uneventful years passed after my dad died. My mom, sister, and I were living in different cities, so we maintained the kind of relationship with which my mom was most comfortable by regular brief Sunday afternoon check-in phone calls and occasional visits.

Then, one Sunday afternoon, my sister and I each got a phone call from my mom that was nearly as monumental as the one my mom received back in 1957. "I think I have pneumonia, and I'm going to the hospital," she told us in turn. I asked her if she wanted one or both of us to come to south Florida where she was living. She didn't hesitate for a moment before answering softly, "Yes."

When we arrived at the hospital, we learned that she didn't have pneumonia. She had breast cancer that had metastasized to her lungs and bones. She'd known she'd had breast cancer for at least two years and had chosen not to tell anyone or to seek treatment. She gave a few halfhearted answers about why she'd made this decision ("I didn't want them to put a tube down my throat to have surgery"), but they didn't add up.

As she signed the papers to enter hospice care in the days following her terminal diagnosis, she began to express two heartbreaking regrets. "I should have gotten treatment. I should have told someone."

They were the first regrets I'd ever heard my mom voice.

All Is Meaningless?

If you want to find a book of the Bible echoing with the sound of regret, it is Ecclesiastes. The book does not claim an author, save "a Teacher" or "a Preacher," depending on your translation. This sage voice comes from someone who identifies himself as a son of David. Many Christian traditions have attributed some or all of the words of Ecclesiastes to Solomon, though many conservative scholars believe the book could have been written several generations later.

Whether it was Solomon or one of Solomon's great-great-great-grandsons, the words of the book were written by someone who had every opportunity to savor all that life offered—and found all of it entirely unsatisfying:

> I denied myself nothing my eyes desired; I refused my heart no pleasure. My heart took delight in all my labor, and this was the reward for all my toil. Yet when I surveyed all that my hands had done and what I had toiled to achieve, everything was meaningless, a chasing after the wind; nothing was gained under the sun. Then I turned my thoughts to consider wisdom, and also madness and folly. What more can the king's successor do than what has already been done? . . . For the wise, like the fool, will not be long remembered; the days have already come when both have been forgotten. Like the fool, the wise too must die! (Eccles. 2:10-12, 16)

He, too, expresses the sentiment that perhaps it was better never to have been born, than to live in a world where oppression and pain seem to win the day, every day (4:1-3). His minor key refrain that everything is meaningless repeats throughout the book.

The Preacher counsels his hearers away from romanticizing the glories of the past when the present becomes too painful: "Do not say, 'Why were the old days better than these?' For it is not wise to ask such questions" (7:10).

Or is it?

He is counseling against sour nostalgia in favor of a different kind of remembering. The final words of the book redirect hearers toward the Lord: "Remember your Creator in the days of your youth, before the days of trouble come and the years approach when you will say, 'I find no pleasure in them'" (12:1). The next eight verses of this chapter go on to describe the bitterness of aging. It is a bitterness soaked to the skin by words of regret. The kind of remembering to which the Preacher calls us in response has more in common with renewing a marriage vow than it does with remembering where you left your car keys.

The epilogue of Ecclesiastes reminds us that God knows well the places of pain and unforgiveness we have hidden behind the divided places on the far side of our hearts: "Fear God and keep his commandments, for this is the duty of all mankind. For God will bring every deed into judgment, including every hidden thing, whether it is good or evil" (12:13-14).

The pain of regret is meant to peel back the packaging covering those hidden things from our view. It is pain from which my mom fled throughout her life until she could run no further.

On the Hook

There was no magic moment in those final, waning weeks of her life in which she came to terms with the lies she'd been told, the rejection she'd experienced, and the deep sense of loss she was unable to name. Once the secret of the cancer she'd kept hidden for more than two years was revealed, her physical condition deteriorated very rapidly.

The one thing she'd withheld from just about every person in her life was the single thing she wanted more than anything else in the waning hours of her life—forgiveness. That longing for mercy drew me to Jesus as a teen. And it was mercy I saw at work in a way I never could have imagined for all of the years since then when a hymn-singing hospice nurse prayed with my mom to receive her Savior's forgiveness. A few days later, at age sixty-eight, she died.

Following her death, I had to come to terms with the ways in which regret—my mom's and my own—affected my life. Many of us who experience difficult childhoods make solemn vows to ourselves that things will be different when we become parents. I know I did.

"If Only's" Corollary: It'll Be Different for Me

With single-minded purpose from the day I first learned I was pregnant with our first child, I worked with the intensity of a tiger mom to keep my own childhood pain out of our home. I wanted my kids to know they were loved and treasured. I wanted them to know they were safe. Most of all, I wanted them to know that the mercy found in Christ was theirs. I expended tremendous amounts of energy in single-minded pursuit of those worthy goals.

Though I'd long ago forgiven my parents, I'd never really considered the lingering effect the message had on me that I was a disappointment and a failure. I just knew I had to protect my kids from it no matter what. The day-in, day-out demands of the active parenting years don't always leave a lot of spare time for reflection.

The time came in the months after my mom died. Both of my sons left the nest during that time, and my daughter and her family, who'd moved home for a season after being out on their own, moved out again as well.

My empty nest echoed with the sound of regret.

It wasn't just the "Sunrise, Sunset" ache at the passing of time most parents feel when they see the baby they cradled in their arms like thirteen minutes ago is all grown up. Most parents experience the challenge of watching their children leave the nest. Some don't immediately soar into the great blue sky. Part of the letting go journey for parents means coming to terms with their own "if only" list as they realize how quickly the years have flown and that there is no possibility of a do-over for their kids' lives or their own.

My regrets went far beyond those. I was filled with dozens of "if onlys" and a heaping helping of self-recrimination when I saw my kids struggle, as many young adults do, with the tasks of building their adulthoods. If only I would have been a better mother, maybe they wouldn't be having problems finding their respective vocational paths. If only I would have made different parenting choices, maybe they wouldn't be struggling with their finances. If only I would have listened better to this question or that conversation during their teens, then all of their relationships now would be guaranteed to be peaceful and happy. If only I would have learned to pick my battles better, they wouldn't be struggling to make their faith their own. If only I could have relaxed a little, then their lives wouldn't seem so complicated. If only. If only. If only.

Ifonlyifonlyifonly.

My "if onlys" scurried in circles like hamsters on wheels in my heart where regret lived. No matter how many ways I apologized to my kids and my husband for any real and/or imagined parenting failures I could remember, I never felt a sense of relief. My husband said to me on numerous occasions, "It sounds as though you've forgotten that I was their parent too. We were in this together, making parenting decisions every step of the way." It was true, but his words brought me no comfort.

I'd long labored under a yoke of responsibility that had never been mine to shoulder, beginning with the responsibility I'd always felt to try to please my deeply wounded mom. That responsibility then shifted in adulthood to include working double-overtime to keep the effects of my painful childhood far, far away from my children.

Eventually, I realized that they weren't the ones from whom I needed to receive forgiveness. I needed to let myself off the hook—a hook on which I'd lived my entire life. While under my parents' roof, I was wounded by my mom's unresolved regret. As a teen, I hoped that receiving Christ's forgiveness would magically shield me from its effects. As a young adult, I thought the spiritual thing was to bury that regret in busyness, and I managed to rack up plenty of new regrets in the process. God used the loss and transition of midlife to help me face all of it—and reconcile with my past—at last.

Get Out of Jail Free

In speaking of God's eternal judgments, the Preacher notes in Ecclesiastes 3:15, "Whatever is has already been, and what will be has been before; and God will call the past to account." In ways we don't even realize, we who live shackled to our "if onlys" are already calling our past to account every day.

What if regret is our Redeemer's gift to us? When he brings the past to our active remembrance, he does so out of his love for us. If our story were over, done, finito at the point of each regret, our lives would indeed be meaningless and without hope of redemption.

People end up in prison because of a crime committed, not because of what they may do in the future. When Jesus told those assembled in his hometown synagogue that he was the fulfillment of the messianic promise found in Isaiah 61, and that he would set captives free (Luke 4:18-19), he was proclaiming, among other things, that regret was not meant to have the final word in our lives. When he himself emerged from the prison of the tomb at his resurrection, he became our way forward, out of death and all of death's imprisoning effects on our day-to-day lives. This includes regret.

As he exposes our sin and we agree with him in confession, by turning back to him, we are positioned to receive his forgiveness. He calls us to forgive as we've been forgiven (Eph. 4:32). At a very basic level, forgiveness is telling someone who has wronged us that he or she does not have to repay us for what was taken from us.

This includes ourselves. We must release ourselves from the debts of our own past failures, just as Jesus has. Christ was present at the time we did what we now regret, and his mercy was there for you even if you chose not to receive it.

You can receive it now. Right now. He knows exactly who you are, and welcomes you, mistakes and all, into your present.

Reflection Questions

1. How might the regrets of others have affected your childhood and teen years? Have you ever considered their actions toward you in light of their own life experience?

2. The Preacher's words throughout the book of Ecclesiastes express the meaninglessness of life. Do you find those words at odds with the rest of Scripture? Why or why not? How might you respond to him if he were to express these sentiments to you today?

3. How has transition or crisis given you an opportunity to reflect on the past in new ways?

4. What is most difficult for you about forgiving yourself for your past "if onlys"?

Prayer

Redeemer, I come to you knowing the words that I am forgiven by you but recognizing that there are areas of my life in which my own lack of forgiveness for myself has prevented me from fully receiving your mercy. I have heard others say that the past is the past, that your mercy covers it all, and perhaps I conflated the two to mean that my history was meaningless except in terms of telling others how I came to faith in you.

My regrets tell me otherwise.

I come to you here and now and ask you to retell me my story. You have been there each step of my way, even when I didn't recognize you, even when I didn't believe in you, and even when I turned from your gaze and did what seemed right in my own eyes. Please, Father, tell me my story, and in doing so, tell me yours anew.

I need a Preacher to tell me the good news that I am forgiven, to tell me that you don't condemn me.

Help me apply your mercy to my past. If you are using change and loss to excavate that past and reunite my divided heart, give me the strength not to try to run from your work but to cooperate with you in it.

I ask these things in the name of the One who chooses not to hold stones in the palms of his nail-pierced hands. Amen.

TEN

ALL THINGS WORK TOGETHER FOR . . .

THE STORY OF THE SEQUEL TO OUR "IF ONLYS"

> Make the most of your regrets; never smother
> your sorrow, but tend and cherish it till it
> comes to have a separate and integral interest.
> To regret deeply is to live afresh.
> —Henry David Thoreau

Reconciliation with our past "if onlys" changes the way we live here and now, in the present tense. When we are unshackled from our past regrets, we are able to experience shalom even as we walk out the consequences of a poor decision or sinful choice. We are at liberty to follow Jesus out of the prison cell and into the world he loves.

There may be times when those first stumbling steps may make us look a little foolish to others. But if we've faced our fears, a bit of awkwardness is nothing in comparison to the fear that held us in chains for so many years.

The best example of this is a story drawn from news headlines. While the names and party affiliations may change, the story line stays the same. It is the stuff of Hollywood blockbusters and gossip columns.

The plot goes something like this: A young, promising politician—let's call him James—has a secret life. He's having an affair, and he has a little recreational cocaine habit. James needs to fund this crazy lifestyle of his, so he "borrows" money from his campaign fund. The money, sex, drugs, and political power are a potent cocktail that anesthetizes his conscience.

That conscience is slapped into wakefulness when a blackmailer who is only interested in selling his services to the highest bidder shows James he has proof of his many indiscretions.

James, then, decides he must be the highest bidder. This decision traps him in a cycle of paying the thug, then paying and paying and paying some more. Whenever James tries to end the relationship, his blackmailer threatens to take the evidence to the press. James's existence is ruled by fear and the need to keep feeding the bottomless pit of the extortionist's demands for cash.

If this were a movie, the story would go one of two ways. Either James would kill the thug, or James would refuse to pay, and the man would go ahead and do what he's been threatening to do all along.

A third option awaits, but no studio head would likely ever green-light this kind of story. James could go to his colleagues and the press and confess it all, hanging every last scrap of dirty laundry on the line. He knows it will end his career and ruin his reputation, but living with his secrets and the threat of exposure is suffocating him.

James chooses the third option. The story makes headlines for a couple of weeks. After the headlines fade, there are consequences of all kinds waiting for the former politician in the wake of his resignation. But the fears that controlled James as if he were a marionette for most of his adult life—both the brokenness that led him to make so many bad decisions in the first place as well as the fears of exposure—no longer have the final word in the way he lives.

As the credits of this movie roll, audiences can see that James is at peace. What will happen next in his life? All kinds of new, hopeful possibilities await.

A sequel is in the making.

What If They Find Out Who I Really Am?

Our regrets whisper to us that the world will find out what kind of people we really are. If others find out the truth about us, will rejection follow? Fear holds us captive.

The shalom of Christ removes the chains from us. The peace he gives to us flows out of his love for us: "There is no fear in love. But perfect love drives out fear, because fear has to do with punishment. The one who fears is not made perfect in love" (1 John 4:18). As we receive his peace, his perfect love for us has the power to banish the fear our regrets hold over us.

Unresolved past regrets will deplete our ability to live in the present. Shalom is not just making peace with our past. Shalom allows us to live with courage and confidence right now. Because of Christ, our regrets do not get to have the final word about who we are today.

Joseph's story offers us a remarkable example of this reality. Genesis 37 tells how this grandson of Abraham, son of Isaac had his life stolen from him by his ten jealous brothers, who'd conspired against him with intent to murder him. They instead sold him into slavery and explained his disappearance by telling their father that a wild animal had killed him. The injustices directed at Joseph piled up as he was imprisoned in Egypt for a crime he didn't commit. He languished forgotten in that place before his eventual release into a role of great responsibility in the country (Gen. 38—41). Even so, he wasn't free to return home. And even if he could, how could he go back to a place where his own siblings loathed him enough to exchange his life for the ancient equivalent of pocket change?

A famine in Canaan brought Joseph's brothers to Egypt in search of grain. In a scene with echoes of the parable of the prodigal son (Luke 15:11-32), Joseph reveals his identity to his brothers and forgives them for what they did to him (Gen. 45). The entire family, including father Isaac and the younger brother he'd never met, Benjamin, is reunited in Egypt.

But it wasn't quite "happily ever after" for the brothers. When Isaac died of old age, the ten feared for their lives. Joseph was in a position of great power, sort of a vice president to Pharaoh, and they knew he had every reason under the sun to nurse a grudge against them. They couldn't believe he'd completely forgiven them. I suspect that was because they couldn't forgive themselves for what they'd done to him and for the years of needless grief their father had experienced.

The ten sent Joseph a delicately worded message that most likely wasn't true: "Your father left these instructions before he died: 'This is what you are to say to Joseph: I ask you to forgive your brothers the sins and the wrongs they committed in treating you so badly.' Now please forgive the sins of the servants of the God of your father" (Gen. 50:16-17).

Once they were certain he'd received the message, they went to see Joseph and prostrated themselves in his presence because they feared for their lives. No small irony in the fact that they told their brother they'd be happy to be his slaves.

Joseph's response to them is one of the most beautiful expressions of trust in God and complete forgiveness in all of Scripture: "'Don't be afraid. Am I in the place of God? You intended to harm me, but God intended it for good to accomplish what is now being done, the saving of many lives. So then, don't be afraid. I will provide for you and your children.' And he reassured them and spoke kindly to them" (vv. 19-21).

Meant for Good

With Joseph's story in mind, Preacher F. B. Meyer asked,

We are apt to see a malicious meaning; are we equally apt to detect the Divine and benevolent one? Our enemies are many, and they hate us with perfect hatred; they are ever laying their plots, and working their unholy purposes. But there is one greater and wiser than they, who, through all these plottings, is prosecuting His Divine purpose. There is another and deeper meaning than appears to the short sight of sense.[1]

Commentator David Guzik noted, "[Joseph] plainly declared, 'You meant evil against me.' Although this was true, it was not the greatest truth. The greatest truth was 'God meant it for good.'"[2]

The apostle Paul told his friends in Rome much the same thing: "And we know that in all things God works for the good of those who love him, who have been called according to his purpose" (Rom. 8:28). The Message paraphrase adds a fresh shading of meaning to these oh-so-familiar words: "Every detail in our lives of love for God is worked into something good."

Many people drain the eternity from this truth with a generic, "It all worked out for the best." But even among believers, the idea that God is at work in everything—everything!—for the benefit of those who have responded to his call with their love sounds suspiciously like something a motivational speaker might say. Perhaps because the words have been overused and misapplied, or perhaps because our present reality may lead us to wonder if this really is what all things working together for our good means, we may be tempted to dismiss this truth. Misapplied sentiments grate against our regrets—and rightly so.

Paul (who knew his share of suffering after his Damascus-road experience) and Joseph (who lived most of his adult life as either a slave or a prisoner) each had plenty of reasons to have questioned God's goodness. Their words were forged on the anvil of years of affliction. They were not speaking motivational platitudes. They were speaking trust. This trust helped them forgive those who'd wronged or hurt them. This trust invited shalom into what could have become quite a collection of "if onlys."

And because shalom existed in their lives, both Joseph and Paul were free to speak and act in ways that reflected the character of God.

All Things New

A few years ago, a young woman came to me and asked me to mentor her. I instantly compiled a lengthy list titled "Why I Would Make a Crummy Mentor." Not surprisingly, almost every single item on the list was some variation of my old "if onlys." (Old habits die hard.)

I shared a few items from my list and gently suggested that she might want to find someone with less past baggage to journey with her.

She pushed back. "But you're willing to talk about your mistakes and show me how God is working with you through them," she said.

Her words were a shock—a happy surprise. Yes, absolutely, I told her. I am willing to share my "if onlys" and the journey through them because God really can and will make all things new. *All things.* Including our regrets.

Her words were like a mile marker of sorts for me. I was learning that I no longer needed to keep my regrets stashed in shame behind a dividing wall in my heart. My regrets are no longer sequestered behind bunkers. They are a part of who I am. They've become a part of my testimony of Christ's redemptive love that I have the privilege of sharing with others.

The apostle Peter emerged from an experience of regret with this kind of testimony. Peter—a poster boy for anyone who acts first and thinks later—spent three years in Jesus' inner circle.

At the final Passover meal Jesus shared with his disciples, right after Jesus told his disciples that everyone would recognize that they belonged to him if they loved one another the way he loved them (John 13:34-35), he told them he would be leaving them. Peter told Jesus he'd lay his life down for him.

Jesus responded to Peter's expression of fidelity by telling him, "Will you really lay down your life for me? Very truly I tell you, before the rooster crows, you will disown me three times!" (John 13:38).

Which is exactly how it went down that night (Matt. 26:69-75). Just before the rooster's call pierced the dawn, Peter insisted for a third time that he didn't know Jesus. The sound brought back the words of Jesus, and Peter sobbed in self-recrimination. How could he turn so quickly on the best friend he'd ever have? How? There couldn't have been any other words scrolling across Peter's broken heart except "if only."

At some point, Peter headed north from Jerusalem, to Galilee, and went back to fishing for a living, which is what he was doing before Jesus called him to follow him three years earlier. He knew Jesus was sentenced to death, and had possibly heard about his resurrection, but he must have assumed his denials of knowing Jesus disqualified him from doing anything more than watching from afar—and remembering.

John 21 tells the story of Peter's reunion with Jesus. Jesus restored him to ministry after doing some major repair work on Peter's divided heart. Jesus asked Peter three times if Peter loved him (vv. 15-17). Each time, Peter replied in the affirmative to this question. Jesus three times asked Peter to care for Jesus' cherished sheep, a nod to the role to which Jesus had called Peter earlier in his ministry (Matt. 16:18).

The third time Jesus asked Peter the question, it broke Peter. Jesus silenced every single one of his "if onlys" with two words.

"Follow me!" (John 21:19).

Peter's remorse led him to assume his actions the night Jesus was arrested were grounds for demotion or dismissal. Instead, they became the launch pad for his sequel. The rest of his life was characterized by Holy Spirit-empowered leadership. If we have been called to follow Jesus out of the prison of our regrets, then he will use all things—including our poor choices and the painful ways in which the sins of others have affected our lives—for his redemptive purposes.

Reflection Questions

1. What kind of story would you write if you were scripting politician James's sequel?

2. As you reflect on the story of Joseph found in Genesis 37—50, in what ways do you see that Joseph's brothers have been imprisoned by their regrets?

3. How might the regret that hurts the most in your life be used for the benefit of someone else?

4. If that regret no longer had a voice of authority in your life, how would this change your present circumstances?

Prayer

Thank you, Lord, that your mercies are new every morning. Thank you, Lord, for sequels, for second acts, for new leaves and fresh starts.

Thank you that as your peace reconnects the pieces of my regret-divided heart, I discover what your word means when you tell me that what was meant for evil against me can be used for good.

Nothing is wasted with you, Father—not a single bit. Even the most cringe-inducing moments from my past can be a gift to others. It may be that the story you're writing in my life will encourage them or point them toward you. It may be that because my heart is being united to honor you, I will respond with greater maturity to those you've placed in my life today.

But I thank you, too, for the way your shalom is expanding my soul. I can sing this snatch of one of King David's songs; his words are my melody to you too: "He reached down from on high and took hold of me; he drew me out of deep waters. He rescued me from my powerful enemy, from my foes, who were too strong for me. They confronted me in the day of my disaster, but the LORD was my support. He brought me out into a spacious place; he rescued me because he delighted in me" (Ps. 18:16-19).

You save me. You love me. And peace in you gives me new freedom to follow you, Jesus. There is nowhere else I'd rather be than here, Savior.

ELEVEN

RUNNING WITH THE PACK

WHEN EVERYONE IS (JUST A LITTLE BIT) RESPONSIBLE, NO ONE IS RESPONSIBLE

Regret is the sound of the ghosts of our own making.

—T. A. Webb

It was an icy Thursday morning shortly before Christmas when Donna's supervisor called her into his office.

"Shut the door behind you," he said. He fidgeted with some papers on his desk and gestured for her to sit down. "Look, Donna, there's no easy way to tell you this. Your position is being eliminated. I'm sorry."

Just a few months short of her fifty-ninth birthday, she was laid off from the corporation where she'd worked for more than a decade. She had a stack of excellent performance reviews; she'd recently received a bonus in recognition of a job well done. A round of emails and phone calls from her former co-workers all echoed the same message: "You didn't deserve this! How could they have laid off a hard worker like you?"

Donna grieved; her shock melted into sadness, which gave way to anger. The anger left her raw and irritated with herself: "If only I'd have taken on that big project last year. If only I'd have learned to play politics better. If only I'd have seen this coming. If only . . ."

Her anger shifted away from herself as she thought about the "they" that had gathered in an office on the far side of the country and made a decision about her. She learned that she was one of eighty people in her division, many of whom were older workers in her age range, who were told their services were no longer needed, each one of them erased from the organizational chart by higher-ups sitting in a sterile conference room. The move was meant to improve the company's bottom line and keep the stockholders happy. Donna wondered if any of the decision-makers felt remorse at having to send eighty people to their local unemployment offices.

I suspect most or all of them did. Some probably lost sleep over the issue. The needs of the thousands of shareholders who counted on the income from dividends were at odds with keeping these high-overhead older employees on the payroll. However, because a number of people were involved in the decision-making process, and these people were acting on behalf of a corporation and not as individuals, each person's sense of discomfort at having to erase names from the org chart was diluted among the entire group like a pint of ink spilled into an ocean.

None of Us Are Islands

Sometimes businesses, organizations, governments, churches, or other groups create policies that leave a trail of hurt and regret in their wake in the lives of individuals. Those who belong to these organizations may be called to do things in the name of the group they'd never imagine doing in their personal lives. Think of a government with a record of human rights violations, for example. The people acting as agents of that government may brutalize others when they're "on the clock," so to speak, but in their private lives, they wouldn't dream of hurting a fly. Or consider an industry covering up their discovery that one of the ingredients in their most popular product causes cancer. Those who know the truth may be otherwise wonderful people who choose to look the other way so they can remain employed and provide for their families.

As long as humans are involved, sin can play a role among any group. However, some groups are intentional about Golden Rule-based practices and policies that keep the organization moving in a healthy direction. On the other hand, some institutions ferment and formalize sin. Group sin has a personality all its own. It compels members to snap to it and conform to the group's rule by playing on variations of fear. That fear can take the form of social pressure, shaming, labeling those who aren't "team players" and eventually forcing them out of the organization. Though Donna could never prove it, she suspected that her age disqualified her from staying on the team at work.

While we are ultimately responsible to God as individuals, none of us are islands. Unless we live a hermit's life, we are a part of various communities, including family, church, work, school, and neighborhood. God also deals with people groups. God chose Israel, a specific people group to reflect his light to the nations (Isa.

49:6). The Old Testament shows the effects of sin permeating the culture and drawing the Israelites away from their mission. God's discipline of them included attacks and invasions by enemy people groups, enslavement, privation, and dispersion. (Of course, the Old Testament also tells us what it looks like when the chosen people repented and returned to that calling. An especially powerful account of return can be found in the books of Ezra and Nehemiah.) God also dealt with the particular sins and strengths of nations surrounding Israel. Jonah's story is one example.

As God drew all the world into his mission through the life, death, and resurrection of Jesus (Matt. 28:18-20), we can see how God continues to speak to particular groups in specific times and locations about their corporate sins and strengths. Think New Testament epistles or the churches named in Revelation 2—3.

Circling the Wagons

Two decades ago, my family was part of a church where the leadership team intentionally covered up the popular lead pastor's affair and his longstanding porn habit. I suspect they hoped to assist in turning him around while allowing him to continue in his position so as not to put the congregation through any trauma. They may have thought they were protecting the pastor, but ultimately, they were protecting their own positions and their reputations. Exposing him would have meant exposing their own leadership compromises. They formed a human shield around a wolf in pastor's clothing, instead of protecting the sheep. Each individual leader seemed to be a mature, wonderful person. But as a group, they became something else.

Anyone who got too close to the truth during the years this occurred was demonized. I once wrote a play for the church about a fictional pastor who focused on building his own kingdom and missed the needs of the marginalized in his own community. It was meant to be a modern parable reminding the congregation to notice and care for all who God brought into our shared life. I had no idea what was going on in the inner circle of the leadership team at the time, though God did! The pastor flew into a rage when I shared the script with him and a small group of others. Instead of apologizing, he branded me the problem, and the rest of the leadership team quickly followed suit. After we spent more than a year trying to work through the issue and its ensuing fallout, my family ended up leaving the church.

At first, I blamed myself. If only I hadn't written those words. If only I would have quietly agreed that I was a problem when the pastor, who I respected deeply, told me so. We saw the same pattern of sin (social pressure, shaming, labeling, and forcing out) repeated with anyone the leadership team perceived as a threat to the status quo. Many from the congregation followed their lead. While the phone calls from those who were experiencing the effects of the sin of the church's leaders validated my own hard experience, there was no joy in their reports for me. If only my husband and I would have recognized the signs of sickness in the church sooner, maybe we could have avoided the whole painful mess.

I am glad to report that my regret dissipated over time as the sad story about the pastor's secret sin became public knowledge. God taught us much about what makes a church's culture toxic, lessons that carried us when we witnessed a split in another congregation of which we were a part a number of years later. We discovered that corporate sin comes with the temptation to disperse its effects among the group's members in such a way that if everyone is responsible, then maybe no one is *really* responsible. Though the truth about the pastor's secret life eventually came to light, none of the leaders who'd protected him all those years lost their position as a result.

As one, they insisted without a drop of remorse they all needed to stay in their posts in order to protect the sheep now that the pastor was gone.

It Can Happen

The apostle Paul confronted a group who'd allowed members involved in an incestuous relationship to continue to be a part of the fellowship. In 1 Corinthians 5, Paul challenges the church to expel this person (vv. 5, 13) in order to bring him to repentance. He notes in the following chapter that sin had gone viral among them, as witnessed by the fact that members were dragging one another into civil court. Jesus' call for his followers to love one another in the self-sacrificing way in which he loved them had been distorted in Corinth in both warped forms of intimacy and in bitter feuds that divided them. It is to these people that Paul penned the ultimate refresher course on what the Lord wanted from them—the "love chapter" in 1 Corinthians 13.

When he wrote his friends in the church a few months later, his verbal discipline had done its cleansing work among them. The church and the individual had both repented, and Paul had the joy of coaching the church toward a regret-free restoration (2 Cor. 2:5-11). He told them they were the ones in this broken world who were called and equipped to broadcast God's message of shalom:

Therefore, if anyone is in Christ, the new creation has come: The old has gone, the new is here! All this is from God, who reconciled us to himself through Christ and gave us the ministry of reconciliation: that God was reconciling the world to himself in Christ, not counting people's sins against them. And he has committed to us the message of reconciliation. (2 Cor. 5:17-19)

It is possible for a group, an organization, a church, even a business or government to repent. A group's "if only" will lead to change. Every member of a particular group will not feel equal remorse over their past errors, but the organization as a whole can change the way in which it behaves. It begins as individuals in a group own their role in perpetuating the group's sin, as the incestuous couple in Corinth did. Most of us have played a part in an unhealthy group, whether it was hanging around with a bunch of mean girls in junior high or "just doing our job" at work and hurting a co-worker or customer in the process.

Group "if onlys" mean that leaders and followers alike become intentional about embracing repentance as a group; it is evidenced by changing the culture that allowed sin to flourish as the congregation in Corinth had. It is possible, because in Christ, "all things are possible" (Matt. 19:26).

Most of us discover that though this is possible, it is uncommon. I think this precious rarity points to a greater reality. For those of us who call Jesus our Lord, we are members of his kingdom. This community is not subject to our politics, power plays, and passions. Jesus used all sorts of images to help us see beyond our own experience so we'd recognize what it looks like to be a part of the community defined by his just and loving rule:

- Healthy (Matt. 13:24)
- Impossible sanctuary (Matt. 13:31-32)
- Transforming (Matt. 13:33)
- Treasure beyond compare (Matt. 13:44-46)
- Characterized by trust, simplicity, and true humility (Matt. 18:3; 19:14)
- Not a meritocracy (Matt. 20:16)
- Fruitful (Matt. 21:43)
- Near, present, and possible in our here and now; not yet fully realized (Matt. 25; Luke 22:15-18)
- Populated with those who experience and share his healing and wholeness (Luke 9:11)
- A paradox: a narrow door (Luke 13:24) and a great banquet (Luke 13:29)
- Embedded within us by the work of the Holy Spirit (Luke 17:21; John 14:26)
- Invisible to those who have not been born again (John 3:3)
- Unlike any group, organization, business, or government we know in this world (John 18:36)

- A wholehearted life of righteousness, shalom, and joy (Rom. 14:17)

The regrets we may accumulate as we respond to the toxic actions of a group can point us toward a deeper desire, the kind of desire that can give us the courage to speak up, walk away, stand with those at the margins, speak the truth, shine a light, and live his shalom as we pray the words Jesus gave his disciples: "Your kingdom come" (Matt. 6:10). Author Frederick Buechner said, "The Kingdom of God is where we belong. It is home, and whether we realize it or not, I think we are all of us homesick for it."[1]

Our "if onlys" connect us with that homesickness.

Reflection Questions

1. What is the most frustrating or hurtful experience you've ever had as the result of a group's behavior or policies? Who do you forgive when an organization's systemic sin has affected your life?

2. Have you ever seen an example of group/corporate repentance? What did it look like? What were the aftereffects of these actions?

3. As you consider the way in which you've been affected by the actions of a group, what regrets do you have?

4. Which image of God's kingdom from the list at the end of the chapter most resonates with you? Why?

Prayer

O Jesus, God with us, when I think about your kingdom, I often revert to believing I can't experience it until after I die or when you return. My images of your kingdom are clouded by what I know of human institutions. I have been at varying times both perpetrator and victim. Group sin and peer pressure and politicking loom large before me; I see your kingdom "through a glass, darkly" (1 Cor. 13:12, KJV).

I think I am homesick.

Yet you say that as we love you with our obedience to you, you will come to us and make your home with us (John 14:23). Your kingdom is *this close*. When I pray that your kingdom comes and your will is done on earth as it has been done in heaven, I am asking for you to reign in me, my Lord.

My obedience to you won't leave an "if only" behind, even when it doesn't change the outcome of the unjust actions done to me by a group. Yet obedience is the way in which my undivided heart responds to all you are. It changes me. It changes the way I respond to the hurtful actions of others, and it changes the way I move and speak by your love when I am a part of a group.

Thank you, Father, for inviting me by your Spirit to be a part of a forever kingdom of no regret about which Jesus showed and told with every moment of his perfect life. Amen.

CONCLUSION
LETTING GO

No space of regret can make amends for
one life's opportunity misused.
—Charles Dickens

In her memoir *The Top Five Regrets of the Dying: A Life Transformed by the Dearly Departing*, Australian hospice worker Bronnie Ware categorized the regrets she'd heard from the lips of the dying throughout the years. These regrets included:

- Living life dependent on the approval of others
- Working too hard
- Lacking the courage to express feelings
- Losing touch with friends
- Not allowing oneself to feel happy

Dr. Karl Pillemer, a professor of human development at Cornell University, noted he was quite surprised by one of the top regrets mentioned by the twelve hundred elderly people he and his team surveyed. Again and again, those surveyed reported that they wished they'd given less of their lives over to worry. Dr. Pillemer wrote, "From the vantage point of late life, many people felt that if given a single 'do-over' in life, they would like to have all the time back they spent fretting anxiously about the future."[1]

Regret is a thief. It steals your life from you.

Wearing the Chains

When we first meet the character Ebenezer Scrooge at the beginning of Charles Dickens' beloved 1843 novella *A Christmas Carol*, he is known around town for his miserly ways. His longsuffering employee, Bob Cratchit, must work in the cold because Scrooge is too cheap to light a fire. Shortly before the holiday, he shuts down his nephew's attempts to invite him once again to a Christmas day gathering with a blistering "Bah, humbug!"

He falls into a restless sleep that night in his dark, gloomy home and is visited by the ghost of his former business partner and kindred spirit, Jacob Marley. Marley is wearing the chains of a prisoner, and he lets Scrooge know that he is now doomed to wander earth in those shackles after death because of the way he lived his life: "I wear the chain I forged in life. . . . I made it link by link, and yard by yard; I girded it on of my own free will, and of my own free will I wore it." He tells Scrooge he wants to spare him from this same horrible eternity, and he promises to send three spirits who will help Scrooge see the true cost of his selfish ways. Unbelieving Scrooge waves off the vision and settles into a restless sleep.

Scrooge is visited first by the ghost of his own past Christmases, who takes him on a tour of those seemingly happier times in his life. He experienced the excitement of learning a meaningful career from a benevolent master and the possibility of love with a beautiful young woman. But his nostalgia is cut short by pain as he witnesses again his own father's rejection of him, and by Belle sadly asking to be released from their engagement because she couldn't compete with what was becoming his only true love and sanctuary—money.

Scrooge was shaken but not stirred by this trip down memory lane. He just about talks himself out of considering what it might mean for him in the here and now when the Ghost of Christmas Present next comes to visit him. The ghost takes him first to "visit" his nephew and his wife casually discussing Scrooge's mean-spirited refusal to be a part of their Christmas gatherings. Next, he visits Bob Cratchit's loving but poverty-stricken household, where he sees Cratchit's ailing, crippled youngest son, Tiny Tim, among the rest of the family gathered for their meager Christmas meal. The meal is scraped together out of the painfully low wages Scrooge has deigned to pay his employee. It begins to dawn on him that he is reaping exactly what he's sown in his life.

The Ghost of Christmas Future then comes to visit him. The ghost gives Scrooge a peek at the legacy he's created with his life. Scrooge discovers that no one mourns the passing of a man like him, and he learns every treasure he's hoarded throughout his life is parceled out to others only interested in the stuff. When he inquires of the ghost if what the spirit is showing him are "shadows of the things that will be, or are they shadows of things that may be, only?" His query is met with silence, and at last, Scrooge has the awakening for which Marley's ghost had hoped. "Men's courses will foreshadow certain ends, to which, if persevered in, they must lead . . . but if the courses be departed from, the ends will change."

And Scrooge at last wants to change. He vows to honor the spirit of Christmas generosity throughout the year, and cries, "I will live in the Past, the Present, and the Future. The Spirits of all Three shall strive within me. I will not shut out the lessons that they teach!"

This cherished story is indeed loaded with lessons. Among them, the true cost of unresolved "if onlys." Scrooge's story illustrates the process by which our regrets steal from our present in order to feed the pain of our past while shackling us with chains that keep us from wholeheartedly following Jesus into our future.

But Scrooge's ghosts remind us that they don't have to. Jesus promises us we can live unshackled from those regrets. Unlike Scrooge, who had a single epiphany that transformed past, present, and future in one fell swoop, most of us will discover that freedom from the chains of "if only" happens as we follow Jesus with our sometimes-stumbling steps out of the prison of our "if onlys."

A New Heart

God used the pen and voice of the prophet Ezekiel to tell his people that he'd been with them even while they'd been held in captivity by their enemies: "Therefore say: 'This is what the Sovereign LORD says: Although I sent them far away among the nations and scattered them among the countries, yet for a little while I have been a sanctuary for them in the countries where they have gone'" (11:16). God promises he will again lead them, step by step, toward the home they'd been forced to leave years earlier.

And then he tells them how he will do for them what they'd already proven they weren't able to do for themselves. "I will give them an undivided heart and put a new spirit in them; I will remove from them their heart of stone and give them a heart of flesh. Then they will follow my decrees and be careful to keep my laws. They will be my people, and I will be their God" (vv. 19-20).

Hundreds of years before Ezekiel prophesied, David asked God for an undivided heart so he could live a life reflecting God's holy character (Ps. 86:11). The freedom that comes with the gift of an undivided heart is a means to an end. It is not God's ultimate goal for us.

In fact, the very next lines in Psalm 86 following this request are the words of a man who well knew where that freedom would lead him: "I will praise you, Lord my God, with all my heart; I will glorify your name forever. For great is your love toward me; you have delivered me from the depths, from the realm of the dead" (vv. 12-13).

A whole heart turns our whole life into a song of praise to the One who unites our divided hearts and delivers us from the shackles of sin and shame.

This song of praise sounds like wisdom. When King Solomon described the virtue of wisdom in Proverbs, he noted that knowing and fearing God with the kind of awestruck, humble honor he'd seen modeled by his father, David, was the starting place for a life shaped by perceptive insight and good judgment (Prov. 9:10). The bulk of the book of Proverbs offers us dozens of slice-of-life snapshots like these showing how a wise person is free to respond when confronted with the behavior of a fool:

- "Fools show their annoyance at once, but the prudent overlook an insult" (12:16).
- "A heart at peace gives life to the body, but envy rots the bones" (14:30).
- "When justice is done, it brings joy to the righteous but terror to evildoers" (21:15).

The shalom of Jesus transforms our regrets into wisdom and sets us free to honor God wholeheartedly. Our "if onlys" no longer hold us hostage but become a valued part of who we've been, who we are, and who we are becoming in Christ.

This song of praise reverberates with courage. God has "reconciled us to himself through Christ and gave us the ministry of reconciliation: that God was reconciling the world to himself in

Christ, not counting people's sins against them. And he has committed to us the message of reconciliation" (2 Cor. 5:18-19). We cannot give to others what we ourselves have not first received from him. As he reconciles us to himself, our "if onlys" become the fuel for reconciliation with others and with ourselves. It takes courage to do the work of reconciliation. On the Mount of Olives, in the garden of Gethsemane, Jesus struggled in prayer to the point that "his sweat was like drops of blood" for the strength to surrender to what he knew was coming—sham trials and crucifixion for crimes (all of humanity's!) he didn't commit (Luke 22:44). His undivided heart submitted to his Father's will, and he had the courage to do the work of reconciliation for and in each one of us as a result. He offers us this same kind of courage as well.

This song of praise is written with the lyrics of compassion. The day our first foster child was placed into the waiting arms of her adoptive parents, I may have broken down in the busy restaurant at lunchtime as sorrow brought me face-to-face with the regret that had partitioned my heart for years. I could no longer ignore what I'd buried on the far side of that wall.

That grief was God's compassion at work; a "partially abundant life" was a poor facsimile for the full, overflowing life he had in mind for me. Instead of clutching onto my woulda, coulda, shouldas, I have begun to learn (and am continuing to discover) that as I let go of regret, my open hands have the capacity to receive his love for me and for others. Instead of trying to avoid, silence, rationalize, or hide from my "if onlys," in the company of the Lord I am learning to listen to even the most discordant notes of my regrets. Author Frederick Buechner said, "We cannot live our lives constantly looking back, listening back, lest we be turned to pillars of longing and regret, but to live without listening at all is to live deaf to the fullness of the music."[2]

It is full and lovely music indeed . . . if only we have ears to hear it.

APPENDIX A
COUNSELING Q&A

God will often use another person to help dismantle the dividing walls we erect in our hearts to protect our regrets. This help may come in an informal conversation and/or prayer with a wise, trusted friend, a pastor, other leader, or in a small group. It may come in a more formal church confessional setting as well. Some congregations offer peer counseling; some organizations offer trained listeners committed to discipleship such as Stephen Ministers (www.stephenministries.org) that may be of help as you are coming to terms with an area of regret.

Some regrets (and the consequences) may have left you or someone you know with mental health issues beyond the scope of a caring peer, however. Depression, anxiety, addictions, the lingering effects of trauma, or a sense that you're "stuck" and don't quite know why may require the help of a skilled counselor.

Some Christians wonder if there is something wrong with their faith if they seek professional help. Recognizing our utter helplessness is at the core of our faith (Rom. 3:22-26). When we admit we need God's help, we are inviting our Healer to work in new ways in our lives (Matt. 9:12).

If you sense that you or someone you know may need professional help in order to move toward wholeness, trying to figure out how and where to get started can be an overwhelming prospect. The information here is by no means comprehensive, but the Q and A's below may serve as a launchpad to help you begin to explore the options available to you.

Q. How can I find a good counselor?
A. Referrals are best. If you have friends who've used a counselor's services, ask them. Most pastors keep the names of a few counselors on hand, as well, as they often need to refer people to them. There are also some Web sites you may find of help to get you started. If there is a seminary in your area, you may find that the school's chaplain or department of pastoral care may be able to put you in touch with the names of some good local counselors. If you are looking for a Christian counselor, you may find this how-to article useful: http://www.aacc.net/2010/05/08/choosing-a-christian -counselor/

Q. What's the difference between a biblical (or nouthetic) counselor and a Christian counselor?
A. We often use words like "biblical" and "Christian" interchangeably, so it is understandable that there might be confusion about the difference between the two when it comes to finding a counselor. However, biblical counseling and Christian counseling typically are two different things.

A biblical counselor is someone who focuses solely on applying Bible passages to areas of sin. This type of counseling, also known as nouthetic (from the Greek *noutheteo*, which means "to admonish") counseling, eschews contemporary psychology, insisting that changed behavior will come solely as the truth of Scripture is applied by a person who is out of alignment with the Word of God. These types of counseling services are rarely covered by insurance, and the training and oversight of those practicing this form of counseling varies wildly.

On the other hand, Christian counselors undergo the same type of training and licensure as their secular counterparts. The counselors' goal is to support and strengthen clients as they pursue their individual goals. While the Christian counselors' faith shapes their approach to their work, they also avail themselves of some of the tools of modern counseling. Some Christian counselors may include Scripture and prayer as part of a session with a client; other Christian counselors may not. The services of a licensed counselor are covered by most insurance plans. You'll want to check with your carrier for the particulars; you'll also want to inquire whether the counselor is a part of your insurance network. If you don't have insurance, or if the therapist is not a part of your insurer's network, he or she may be able to either work with your finances or refer you to someone who can.

When I've mentioned counseling in the book you hold in your hands, I am referring to a trained, licensed counselor. There have been a couple of times in my life when I've experienced severe depression, and while applying Scripture, the listening ears of good friends and the prayers of others have all been helpful, the severity and duration of my depression called for the assistance of a trained, professional Christian counselor. God used a wise, experienced counselor to help me identify a couple of long-held regrets that were fueling at least part of my depression, to help me recognize my divided heart, to remind me of the Bible truths I already knew, and to help me rekindle a desire to apply God's Word to all areas of my life.

Q. What if I can't find a Christian counselor?
A. You may live in an area where there aren't any Christian counselors from which to choose. Recognize that God can use a counselor who does not identify as a Christian. A good counselor is supposed to support you as you are, not try to "evangelize" you to his or her belief system. Pastor Adrian Warnock explained,

> Secular counseling works at an altogether different level. Accepting our brokenness, it tries to help us find strategies to get by in this difficult world. Negative thought patterns are challenged. Behaviors that make things worse for us are identified and addressed. Patterns in how we relate to others are discussed. And sometimes, simply a safe place is created where we can be listened to as we speak about how difficult life has

been for us . . . both biblical help and psychological help can be very relevant to people. Actually, sometimes psychological help will get us in a better position to be able to process and understand what the Bible says about our problems.

Whilst sin is ultimately at the root of all our problems, both physical and mental, it is not directly the cause of everything that goes wrong with us. So, most of the time Christians have no problem going to a doctor to help fix a broken leg. Why then do we not like going to a psychologist or psychiatrist if we have a broken mind and/or broken emotions? Such secular help is often invaluable.[1]

Asking a potential counselor about his or her approach to your faith is just as important as finding out about his or her experience with clients who have concerns or issues similar to yours, what his or her counseling philosophy is, or whether he or she can work with your insurance plan.

Q. Where can I find additional resources for myself or for someone I love who may be struggling with mental health issues?
A. This is by no means an exhaustive list, but here are a couple of resources you can use to begin your search for the help you or your loved one deserves:

- National Alliance on Mental Illness (NAMI)—www.nami. org. This grassroots organization is a clearinghouse for all kinds of information about mental illness and offers free local family education, referrals, and support. In addition, NAMI's FaithNet arm is a helpful resource for church leaders who are looking for information about mental health issues in order to better serve their congregations.

- Mental Health Ministries: http://www.mentalhealthministries.net. This ministry's goal is to de-stigmatize mental illness in the church and provide congregations with educational and spiritual tools in order to better serve their congregants and communities.

APPENDIX B

KEY SCRIPTURES FEATURED IN EACH CHAPTER

1. Woulda, Coulda, Shoulda Versus Me:
   Recognizing Regret
   2 Corinthians 7:10

2. Oh, the Places We Go!
   Hiding from the Sins We Commit
   Luke 15:11-32 (part 1); Exodus 32

3. Doing a Whole Lot of Nothing:
   Avoiding the Messes of Others
   Luke 10:25-37; Matthew 25:31-46

4. I Want What I Have and I Want What You Have Too:
   Stealing Your Own Life
   2 Kings 11—12

5. Hiding in a Stack of Fig Leaves:
   When Someone Else's Sin Tries to Write Your Story
   Luke 15:11-32 (part 2)

6. What's in the Vault?
   Compartmentalizing as a Way to Silence the Past
   Mark 5:1-20; Luke 8:26-39; Matthew 8:28-34

7. The Truth, the Whole Truth, and Nothing but the Truth:
   The Confession Cure
   Psalm 51; Jonah 1—4

8. Truce like a River?
   The Peace That Crosses Our Dividing Walls
   John 7:53—8:11; John 14:26-27

NOTES

Introduction

1. Tara Parker-Pope, "What's Your Biggest Regret?" *Well* (blog), *The New York Times*, http://well.blogs.nytimes.com/2011/03/23/whats-your-biggest -regret/?_r=0 (March 23, 2011).

2. Ed Stetzer, "New Research: Bad Choices Burden Americans," *The Exchange* (blog), *Christianity Today*, http://www.christianitytoday.com/edstetzer /2013/october/new-research-bad-choices-burden-americans.html?visit _source=facebook (October 23, 2013).

Chapter 2

1. Henri J. M. Nouwen, *The Return of the Prodigal Son: A Story of Homecoming* (New York: Doubleday, 1992), 43.

2. Gabriel Garnica, "Sin and Rationalization," *Catholic Exchange*, http:// catholicexchange.com/sin-and-rationalization/ (December 31, 2003).

Chapter 4

1. William Barclay, *The Letters to the Philippians, Colossians and Thessalonians*, in New Daily Study Bible, 3rd ed. (Louisville, KY: Westminster John Knox Press, 2010), 176.

2. C. S. Lewis, *The Weight of Glory, and Other Addresses* (New York: Macmillan, 1949).

Chapter 5

1. Brene Brown, *I Thought It Was Just Me but It Isn't: Making the Journey from "What Will People Think?" to "I Am Enough"* (New York: Gotham Books/Penguin Press, 2007), 212.

2. Lewis Smedes, *Shame and Grace: Healing the Shame We Don't Deserve* (San Francisco: HarperOne, 2009), 41.

Chapter 6

1. C. H. Spurgeon, "A Divided Heart" (sermon, Surrey Hall, London, United Kingdom, September 25, 1859).

Chapter 7

1. Martha Beck, "Before You Confess Your Deep, Dark Secrets," *Empower Yourself* (blog), *O, The Oprah Magazine*, http://www.oprah.com/omagazine /Your-Guide-to-Confessing-Your-Deep-Dark-Secrets (June 2002).

2. *Today in the Word* (Chicago: Moody, 1993).

3. Richard J. Foster, *Celebration of Discipline*, 3rd ed. (San Francisco: Harper San Francisco, 2002), 144.

4. Amy Simpson, "Confessions of the Well-Behaved," *Today's Christian Woman*, http://www.todayschristianwoman.com/articles/2013/august/confessions-of-well-behaved.html?start=1 (August 2013), accessed February 3, 2014.

5. Vance Havner, http://www.sermonstore.org/vance-havner/Quotes.html, accessed February 26, 2014.

Chapter 8

1. Dietrich Bonhoeffer, *The Cost of Discipleship* (New York: Touchstone Publishing, 1995), 44.

2. Cornelius Plantinga Jr., *Not the Way It's Supposed to Be: A Breviary of Sin* (Grand Rapids: Eerdmans, 1996), 10.

Chapter 10

1. F. B. Meyer, "February 20," Our Daily Homily, crosswalk.com, http://www.crosswalk.com/devotionals/dailyhomily/our-daily-homily-february-19-11529516.html, accessed February 26, 2014.

2. David Guzik, "Study Guide for Genesis 50," *Blue Letter Bible*, http://www.blueletterbible.org/Comm/guzik_david/StudyGuide_Gen/Gen_50.cfm, accessed February 26, 2014.

Chapter 11

1. Frederick Buechner, *Secrets in the Dark: A Life in Sermons* (New York: Harper Collins Publishers, 2007), 149.

Conclusion

1. Karl D. Pillemer, "The Most Surprising Regret of the Very Old—and How You Can Avoid It," *The BLOG* (blog), Huffington Post 50, http://www.huffingtonpost.com/karl-a-pillemer-phd/how-to-stop-worrying-reduce-stress_b_2989589.html (April 4, 2013).

2. Frederick Buechner, *Listening to Your Life: Daily Meditations with Frederick Buechner* (New York: Harper Collins Publishers, 1992), 4.

Appendix A

1. Adrian Warnock, "Should a Christian Go to Counseling with a Secular Therapist?" *Adrian Warnock* (blog), Patheos.com, http://www.patheos.com/blogs/adrianwarnock/2013/06/should-a-christian-go-to-counseling-with-a-secular-therapist/ (June 6, 2013).

How are you making a difference?

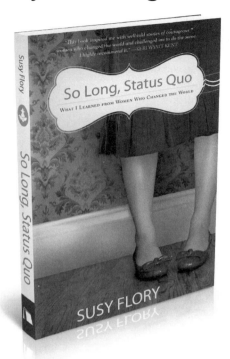

So Long, Status Quo is the powerful story of how nine amazing historical women inspired a suburban mom to abandon her safe, sheltered, vanilla existence for a life of passion, service, and significance. With challenging insight and honesty, Susy Flory shares about her struggles with selfishness and complacency, and tells how the lives of these fascinating women challenged her to get up off her couch and embark on a quest for something more.

Inspiring, convicting, and transformational, *So Long, Status Quo* challenges women to examine their lives and answer this question: What are you doing to get God's work done in the world?

So Long, Status Quo
What I Learned from Women Who Changed the World
SUSY FLORY
ISBN: 9780834124387

BEACON HILL PRESS
OF KANSAS CITY

HOW WILL YOU BE REMEMBERED?

You don't have to be rich, famous, or even dead to leave a legacy. Our legacies are left as imprints on the hearts and minds of those who know us best. The small choices and behaviors we repeat over time is what others will remember long after we've moved, changed jobs, or died.

Your Unforgettable Life examines the impact decisions have on the legacy we leave, and shows how to make wise choices that will result in an unforgettable life.

Your Unforgettable Life
Jennifer Schuchmann, Craig Chapin
ISBN: 978-0-8341-2187-4

BEACON HILL PRESS
OF KANSAS CITY

Available online at BeaconHillBooks.com